# TEACHING
## That Makes a
# DIFFERENCE

## Ronald G. Held

*Thanks!*

*God bless You.*

Developed and Edited by the
National Sunday School Department

*from Virginia Chan*
*CE dept. Lord's Grace Church*

Gospel Publishing House *Sept. 19, 1993*
Springfield, Missouri
02–0664

Library of Congress Catalog Card Number 91–76515
International Standard Book Number 0–88243–664–3
Printed in the United States of America

# Contents

# Contents

# Foreword

Sunday school is as American as apple pie, as hardy as crabgrass, and as taken for granted as a mother's love. Its contributions to the church are many: the transfer of basic life-values to another generation, the consistent systematic teaching of the Bible, and the small-group settings by age-level that permit relationships to develop. Sunday school also undergirds our society through its teaching of ethics, morals, and personal relationships with God and others.

We must maintain the solid principles of Christian education on which Assemblies of God Sunday schools are built. The principles are universal; they are never out of place or outdated. But new methods may be more effective in relating the truth of the Scriptures to our students' lives.

Merely repeating traditions is insufficient. Society has changing problems, and people have differing needs. But God's Word has the answers. We must let God use us to provide biblical solutions to those problems and needs. And we can. God will help us to remain true to biblical truth and sound educational concepts while giving us the freedom to adapt our teaching styles and methods as our students' needs and circumstances change.

One of the key challenges to today's Sunday school is to elevate the ministry of teaching. We must recognize that teaching is a gift to the church and a calling from God. As we place teaching in its proper place in the church, the teacher's image will be elevated in the eyes of the students, the congregation, and the teacher himself. Teachers make a difference. As teachers, we should appreciate our vital role in the church.

In *Teaching That Makes a Difference,* Pastor Ron Held offers one of the most practical ways for elevating the teacher's image—by increasing the teacher's effectiveness. Read and study the text carefully. Allow its practical and spiritual concepts to change both *why* and *how* you teach. As you study age-level development you will be able to better understand the needs of your individual students. As you are introduced to new methods of teaching you will be challenged to become more creative. Using a variety of teaching methods amplifies the students' natural motivation to learn.

Training, coupled with personal commitment, will make you a more effective tool for the Holy Spirit to use in changing your students' lives. And God will truly make you a "teacher who makes a difference!"

GEORGE EDGERLY, SECRETARY
Sunday School Department
Assemblies of God

# 1
# The Purpose of Bible Teaching

Someone has astutely observed that the person who knows how will always have a job, but will always work for the one who knows why. It's vitally important that we as Bible teachers know how to go about our task of teaching the timeless truths of God's Holy Word. This book, for the most part, focuses on the practical aspects of Bible teaching. In this opening chapter, however, we will begin with something more basic and in some ways more important—an understanding of our purpose in Bible teaching.

## Understanding Our Purpose and Mission

As Sunday school teachers and leaders, we tend to know more about the how-tos of our ministry than the whys and wherefores. In fact, we sometimes get so caught up in doing our work for the Lord, that we lose sight of the reason for our efforts. So let's begin by thinking through some of the basic purposes of the Bible-teaching ministries in the local church. We'll focus on the Sunday school's role in particular.

### A MATTER OF BALANCE

Occasionally I am still asked whether the Sunday school's primary ministry is evangelism or education. My stock answer has always been, "Yes." "Yes, the purpose of the Sunday school is evangelism." And, "Yes, the purpose of the Sunday school is education." That may sound a bit like double-talk, but that is unintentional. The question of purpose is not a matter of either evangelism *or* education. The Sunday school's purpose is both evangelism *and* education. Both are essential if our teaching is to make a significant difference in people's lives.

In his 1980 training text, *The Sunday School Spirit,* Steve Rexroat defines Sunday school as an "evangelism-through-education effort."[1] This definition indicates a nice balance. In regard to the growth of First Assembly in Rockford, Illinois, former pastor Ernest J. Moen says, "Evangelism and education are the two wings that fly the airplane. They are indispensable. You reach people, but then you teach them."[2]

The Sunday school must be evangelistic. Its very life depends on that. Whenever a Sunday school turns wholly inward, it loses its zeal and motivation. Research by various church growth organizations indicates the primary difference between growing and declining churches is the degree of emphasis they place on outreach and evangelism. As early as 1963, Herbert W. Byrne said, "Evangelism is the chief work of the Sunday School. In fact, Christian education cannot be Christian unless it is evangelistic. . . . To fail here is to fail in our primary reason for existence and service."[3]

But to go all out for evangelism at the expense of quality education is equally dangerous. Without sound teaching, both converts and established saints fail to grow in their Christian experience. Providing quality ministry in the classroom is one of the best ways to have a growing Sunday school. George Edgerly, national Sunday School Department secretary, has a favorite Iowa story about an old hog farmer who said, "Ya not only gotta get 'em to come to the trough; ya gotta have somethin' for 'em when they get thar."

"Making disciples" is essential and exciting, but "teaching them to obey all things" is also part of the process. In fact, it's a lifelong process requiring quality education at every age-level, from the nursery to the senior adult class. But as you well know, this involves a lot of work. Continual attention must be given to training staff, developing facilities, improving teaching techniques, and using the best resources. Although at times the temptation of simply drawing a large crowd and preaching to everyone at once seems like an easier way to do things, the long-term results are often disappointing and even tragic. Doing the unspectacular and doing it well is usually the best way to get the job done.

Growing churches and Sunday schools know this. They see evangelism and education as two sides of the same coin—both part of a balanced ministry. The Sunday school also provides several other vital ministries in the church. For example, it reaches out in love to those in need, for it not only concerns itself with the students' spiritual needs, but also seeks to minister to their other real-life needs. Sunday school workers are often the first to become aware of people's needs and to take the lead in reaching out to help them. They continue to minister as Christ did to the poor, the brokenhearted, the captives, the blind, and the bruised (Luke 4:18).

The Sunday school also keeps a vital focus on the family, which is at the very heart of the Sunday school. Its ministries to the family begin with the cradle roll and reach all the way to the home extension department. Young children learn faithfulness to God's house. Parent-teen relationships are open for discussion. Dads and moms learn parenting skills. Older adults learn how to prepare for a fulfilling time of retirement. The whole family is blessed by the Sunday school.

UNDERSTANDING OUR MISSION

Having briefly spelled out the balanced purpose for the Sunday school's ministry, let's turn our attention now to developing an understanding of our sense of mission as participants in that ministry.

First, we must define a "sense of mission." Billie Davis defines it as an awareness of one's spiritual giftedness and calling and the "privilege and responsibility of fulfilling a unique part of God's plan."[4] This sense of being one of God's coworkers is important, for it gives meaning to what we are doing. We can see that our efforts are directed toward some purposeful end. As Dr. Davis points out, a teacher's involvement with his students' needs can be exhausting, sometimes to the point of frustration, disillusionment, and self-doubt. "Only the sense of mission—the assurance of divine calling and purpose—can keep teachers genuinely interested, eager, loving, and willing to develop their gifts."[5]

Second, we must develop and maintain a sense of mission by studying God's Word. We must see from a biblical perspective what the ministry of teaching is and its place of importance in God's plan for His church. A sense of mission is often communicated more from spirit to spirit than from mind to mind; therefore, we must spend adequate time in prayer. As we earnestly seek God's will for our lives, He will help us discover the spiritual ministries He has put within us.

Third, we must seek the counsel of leaders within the church who can confirm our call. Their overview of the church's ministries can help us in discovering our place of service.

Fourth, we must gain training and experience. Nothing helps strengthen our sense of mission more than seeing the successful results of our efforts. And nothing helps us succeed like training.

### The Place of Sunday School in the Decade of Harvest

Our Fellowship has undertaken an ambitious plan of growth and expansion for the final decade of the 1990s. Every church agency is being marshaled to help carry out this plan. The Sunday school's purposes and practices equip it to play a vital role in the Decade of Harvest. We can readily see how its ministries can help us reach the four goals we are seeking to accomplish during this 10-year period.

1. *To add 5 million new souls to the kingdom of God*—Our churches today have many ways of reaching out to the lost, but the Sunday school remains an effective outreach and evangelism tool. Students are encouraged to bring unchurched friends and family with them to Sunday school. The plan of salvation is explained at each age-group's level of understanding.

2. *To plant 5,000 new churches*—Many different means are being employed to open new churches, including starting branch Sunday schools, which often form the nucleus for a new church.

3. *To add 20,000 full-time workers to the harvest*—Again, the Sunday school can play a key role in this effort because it provides entry-level experiences for those who feel called into the ministry. Its staff is usually the largest in the church and makes use of a wide variety of talents and abilities (e.g., teachers, helpers, administrators, musicians, secretaries).

4. *To enlist 1 million prayer warriors*—The Sunday school staff and its students are a great force that can be marshaled for this task. What better place is there than the Sunday school to teach and train all age-levels on the importance and power of intercessory prayer?

As you can see, the goals of the Decade of Harvest and the basic purposes of the church's teaching ministries are closely related to the threefold commission Christ gave His followers (Matthew 28:19,20). Let's look in more detail at how the church's teaching ministries relate to each facet of that commission.

EVANGELISM

"Go and make disciples of all nations" (Matthew 28:19, NIV).

The Sunday school has always been a primary outreach and evangelism arm of the Church. Often a new believer's first contact is through the Sunday school or a related teaching ministry like children's church or vacation Bible school. The Sunday school has great potential for outreach and evangelism for several reasons:

1. *The Sunday school can quickly respond to changing needs and situations.* For example, if several immigrants enter the community, a special language class can be organized to minister to them. Or if the shutdown of a major industry occurs, several adult classes can take on the task of providing spiritual counsel and material assistance for affected families.

2. *The Sunday school offers a variety of classes for different*

*interest groups.* Specialized classes can be built into the Sunday school's existing structure as the need arises. For example, a class for engaged couples can be scheduled during the spring to provide valuable premarital training. An adult elective can be offered to provide help for those coping with family members who are struggling with life-controlling habits. Such classes will minister not only to regular attendees, but also to the unchurched—an excellent outreach opportunity.

3. *The Sunday school classroom is an ideal setting for evangelism.* Its smaller, more personal atmosphere is less threatening than a large auditorium or evangelistic crusade. Teachers know more about their students' spiritual needs because they have more contact with them both inside and outside the church. Also, Sunday school lessons provide frequent opportunities to present the plan of salvation. Each age-group can hear the gospel at its level of interest and understanding.

If the Sunday school classroom is such an ideal setting for evangelism, why aren't more students saved there? First, there are often few, if any, unsaved students in the average classroom. Second, some teachers do not know how to present the plan of salvation and call for a decision. And third, many Sunday school teachers do not see themselves as soul winners. If you were to ask them, "Do you see yourself more as an educator or as an evangelist?" most would be quick to respond with the former.

Several ways we can make the Sunday school's evangelism ministries more effective are by promoting outreach activities that will bring more unsaved people into the classroom, by training all teachers in the techniques of classroom evangelism, and by helping teachers see that their role includes both education and evangelism.

4. *The Sunday school provides the church with many prospects for evangelism.* According to the Institute of American Church Growth in Pasadena, California, 79 percent of all people who attend church do so at the invitation of a friend or family member. Just 6 percent come because they like the pastor, 3 percent are walk-ins, and 2 percent come because they have a

special need.[6] This means our students' unsaved and unchurched friends and family members are the best prospects
for outreach ministries. They will usually be more responsive
than the general public because they already know something
about our churches and Sunday schools.

INCORPORATION

"... Baptizing them in the name of the Father and of the Son
and of the Holy Spirit" (Matthew 28:19, NIV).

Water baptism has always been a sign of identification with
Christ and His church. Newly saved and baptized believers
were expected to take their place in the life and ministry of
the Church. We still have a great need for this incorporation
and assimilation process. So many congregations have a "back
door" problem—they bring people in through one door and lose
them through another. The Sunday school and other Bible-
teaching ministries can play a vital role in helping people become established.

1. *The Sunday school can provide opportunities for friendship
and fellowship.* Attending only the worship services does little
to generate close relationships. Involvement in a Sunday school
class, however, offers many opportunities for new people to
make friends. Class socials and other outside activities are
important settings in which friendships can develop. In youth
and adult classes, a preclass fellowship period with coffee and
doughnuts is not a waste of time, but a good way for students
to get acquainted. Every class usually has a few students who
are very effective at helping new people meet others and feel
at home. Such students need to understand they have the ministry gift of hospitality that is so vital to the growth of the
church and the Sunday school.

2. *The Sunday school can provide opportunities for involvement in ministry.* Remember, thrusting forth more people into
full-time ministry is one goal of the Decade of Harvest. The
Sunday school is where individuals can begin to discover, develop, and use their ministry gifts. The importance of involve-

ment was reinforced in a study by a major Protestant denomination. It found that among growing churches there were 60 roles or tasks for every 100 members. Among plateaued churches, there were 40 roles or tasks per 100 members. Declining churches had just 20 roles or tasks per 100. Having a place to plug in to the church's life and ministry is essential in both reaching *and* retaining new people.

The Sunday school is also a good place to teach members about their responsibility to the Body. A study of ministry gifts among youth and adults is an important part of the training process, for it helps people understand where and how they fit into the Church's total mission. Once they gain this understanding and an awareness of their areas of spiritual giftedness, the task of enlisting and motivating them to serve is much easier.

3. *The Sunday school can provide opportunities for commitment and accountability.* People need to learn to be faithful to the church and its ministries. The Sunday school can help them develop a sense of commitment because it has one of the best recordkeeping systems in the church. By closely monitoring the students' attendance patterns, the teacher or evangelism coordinator can quickly initiate appropriate follow-up procedures if problems are noted. If members know they are missed when absent, they tend to be more faithful in attendance. Visitors too need to know their attendance was noticed and appreciated.

EDUCATION

". . . Teaching them to obey everything I have commanded you" (Matthew 28:20, NIV).

Our goals for the Decade of Harvest are not only to see many people make decisions for Christ, but also to see them become disciples of Christ. The discipling process is not complete until the new believers are growing in spiritual knowledge and contributing in some way to the church's growth. This, again, is where the Sunday school's teaching and training ministries come into the picture. The Sunday school's teaching ministry has the following unique characteristics:

1. *Age-level teaching*—The Sunday school is the church's only Bible-teaching agency that reaches all ages and family members. In this specialized setting, the Bible can be taught at each person's level of understanding and experience.

2. *Involvement in the learning process*—In the children's departments, the involvement may take the form of interest centers where kids can engage in a variety of learning activities. Youth and adults can become participants in discussion, writing, classroom projects, and other activities of interest to them. The purpose is not activity for activity's sake, but to motivate the students and strengthen their learning experiences.

3. *A systematic approach to Bible study*—Using a quality curriculum like Radiant Life/Vida Nueva ensures that all the major themes and units of the Bible will eventually be covered. Using a building-blocks approach, the curriculum introduces ideas and concepts appropriate to each age-level. Curriculum writers give careful consideration to each age-group's needs and comprehension ability.

4. *Training for ministry*—Every church has a continual need for more trained workers. Some churches meet that need by scheduling another day and time for training sessions. Yet the Sunday school has great potential for training leaders for the entire church. It may not be necessary to organize another program on another night for an already busy church. It can all be done through the Sunday school.

For example, the midweek boys and girls club programs can have a training session for potential leaders during the Sunday school hour. Evangelism teams, altar workers, ushers, and other church workers can also meet for training at that time.

Younger children can begin to learn their responsibilities to serve the Lord and help reach the lost through programs like the Boys and Girls Missionary Crusade (BGMC). Youth classes can begin studying the ministry gifts, which will help the young people to discover their place of service to the Lord. Older, more mature youth, can serve as occasional helpers in the children's departments or as vacation Bible school workers. Their training for those ministries can begin right in Sunday school with a special short-term training class.

As a Sunday school teacher, you are involved in a vital ministry of the church: its Bible-teaching ministry. Knowing *why* you teach will help you train more effectively in knowing *how* to teach. Remember, your total involvement is all part of helping to fulfill our Master's Great Commission to win the world for Him.

Of course, many things will be required of you as you strive for excellence as a Christian teacher. The rest of this book will help you move toward a quality teaching ministry. A review of needed personal characteristics is a good place to start your quest. Ask the Lord to develop them in your life.

## For Further Study

1. Why is it important that we understand the purpose of the Sunday school's ministry?
2. How would you complete this statement: "The purpose of Sunday school as I see it is . . ."?
3. What do we mean by a "sense of mission"? How do we develop and maintain a sense of mission?
4. How can the Sunday school help the church fulfill the goals of the Decade of Harvest?
5. What makes the Sunday school effective in evangelism?
6. How can you help your church incorporate and assimilate new people into its life and ministry?
7. What is unique about the Sunday school's Bible-teaching ministries?

## NOTES

[1]Stephen Rexroat, *The Sunday School Spirit* (Springfield, Mo.: Gospel Publishing House, 1979), 10.

[2]*Way To Grow* (Springfield, Mo.: National Sunday School Department, 1981), 19.

[3]Herbert W. Byrne, *Christian Education for the Local Church* (Grand Rapids, Mich.: Zondervan Publishing House, 1963), 24.

[4]Billie Davis, *Teaching To Meet Crisis Needs* (Springfield, Mo.: Gospel Publishing House, 1984), 23.

[5]Ibid., 24,25.

[6]"Editorial Perspective," *Ministries Today* 8 (November/December 1990), 16.

# 2
# The Personal Life of the Teacher

Findley B. Edge, the great Southern Baptist Christian educator, says, "The single most important factor that influences learning is the *life and personality of the teacher*"[1] (emphasis is Edge's). To test if this statement is true, ask yourself the following questions: Who were some of my favorite teachers when I was growing up? What do I remember most about them?

Your answers will tend to relate more to the kinds of persons your favorite teachers were than to the things they taught or even how they taught. The same will be true of your students' recollections of you. They will remember you more for who you were than for what you did. As has been noted, we teach some by what we say, more by what we do, but most by what we are.

Any discussion of effective Bible teaching, therefore, must take into account the teacher's personal life. That will be our focus in this chapter. We will consider priorities and motives for teaching, your personal devotional life, and other qualities that will make you a better person, and therefore a better teacher.

## Doing Versus Being

An interesting account in Luke 10:38–42 focuses on the need for determining right priorities in the matter of being versus doing and waiting versus going. It involves the familiar conflict between Mary and Martha over the unexpected visit of Jesus and His disciples. Martha immediately began preparing for her guests, worrying and fretting as she went about her work. Mary, much to her sister's consternation, settled down at Jesus' feet to listen to all He had to say. Finally in frustration Martha asked the Lord to intervene and force Mary to help her.

"Martha, Martha," Jesus said, "you are fretting and fussing about so many things; but one thing is necessary. The part that Mary has chosen is best" (Luke 10:41,42, NEB). What was Mary's choice? It was to put being before doing and waiting before going.

As a Sunday school worker you're a natural doer, aren't you? You're a self-starter; you get things done. As a doer, however, do you sometimes excuse your weakness in one area by pointing to your accomplishments in another? Do you sometimes say, "Well, I'm not the greatest spiritual leader, but I am a good administrator"? Or, "I'm not much of a Bible student, but I can put together a pretty interesting class session"? The fact is, successes in one area do not make up for failures in another. The better choice as a Sunday school teacher is to emphasize being before doing.

Mary was a waiter; Martha was a goer. It doesn't take a lot to figure out how to classify most Sunday school workers. The hardest thing for a goer is to learn to wait. That can be a real problem when it comes to taking time to develop your spiritual life. Like Martha, it's easy to let the pressures of responsibilities crowd out time with God. One of my college professors, Lois LeBar, often said, "The greatest hindrance to devotion to Christ is service for Him."

As Sunday school teachers and leaders, it is best to wait on God for insights into His Word, for help in resolving discipline problems, and for guidance in making decisions. The better choice is to wait before going.

Let's consider in more detail several areas where you may need to establish right priorities as they relate to your work in the Sunday school.

COMMITMENT TO CHRIST

The Bible teaches that a relationship to Christ should be top priority. That means commitment to Christ is more important than commitment to family, church, job, or self. Jesus said, "Seek first his kingdom and his righteousness, and all these things will be given to you as well" (Matthew 6:33, NIV). To the rich young ruler He said, "Go, sell everything you have and give to the poor, and you will have treasure in heaven" (Mark 10:21, NIV).

Before looking for servants to work for Him, the Lord seeks saints to love Him and fellowship with Him. A Sunday school teacher who wants to teach the written Word with effectiveness and power must live in close fellowship with the Living Word.

## COMMITMENT TO THE BODY OF CHRIST

Your first commitment is to God, but your second is to others in the body of Christ. The New Testament has more to say about believers' relationships to one another and to the world than about the work they are to carry out. Jesus emphasized this when He defined the identifying mark of His followers: "By this all men will know that you are my disciples, if you love one another" (John 13:35, NIV).

Your relationship to your family should be of primary concern to you as a Sunday school worker. The Bible contains the accounts of many great leaders who accomplished much for God, but provided poor leadership in their own families. Eli, the high priest, was a devoted priest, but a defective parent. The prophet Samuel and King David were also substandard parents. Someone has paraphrased Mark 8:36 to read: "What shall it profit a Sunday school teacher if he win his entire class to Christ, but lose his own children?"

Admittedly, a delicate balance exists between your commitment to the church's work and your commitment to your own family. It is possible for your family to keep you from effectively serving the Lord. But all too often church leaders sacrifice their families for the good of the church and its ministries.

Responsibility to the work of the church has been emphasized so strongly, some people feel guilty if they are not involved at church several nights a week. Wise church leaders who realize their people need more time at home together try to schedule at least one or two family-at-home nights each week. One pastor's wife was heard to say, "Someone else can teach my Sunday school class. Someone else can play the piano. Someone else can bring refreshments for the ladies' luncheon. But I'm the only one who can be a mother to my children."

## COMMITMENT TO THE WORK OF CHRIST

Your love for the Lord just naturally leads to obedience to Him (John 14:15), and obedience to Him leads to a desire to serve Him. Christ's Great Commission to His followers was a commission to work for Him. Jesus said He had come to do the work His Father had sent Him to do (John 9:4). He also said those who believe on Him would do even greater works than He did (John 14:12). God has chosen to accomplish His work through His people. That is His plan for reaching the world with the gospel message.

Christian service, then, is the responsibility of every believer, not just the 20 percent who end up doing 80 percent of the work. Paul said the body of Christ grows when every member does his part (Ephesians 4:16). Your commitment to the Lord and to one another does not excuse you from your commitment to the work of Christ. To be a Christian is to be involved in all three levels of priority.

Understand, of course, there are no easy answers to the problem of priorities. You must constantly work at maintaining the right priorities. And what may be right for one person may not be right for another. So you must guard against forcing your set of priorities on someone else. Everyone, however, is responsible to the Lord.

## Motives for Teaching

Sometimes it is good to think about your motives for teaching. Ask yourself these questions, Why do I teach Sunday school?

What motivates me as a worker? Your answers will help sharpen your focus.

Author Lawrence O. Richards says people teach for many different reasons.[2] Some do so out of a sense of duty. They feel they ought to support the church's ministries. Besides, they know how difficult it is to enlist enough teachers, so they dutifully shoulder their share.

Others teach out of friendship or as a personal favor to the pastor or another leader. Still others serve because they got started years ago and can't find a way to gracefully bow out. Some do it because they like the pastor and others to look up to them. Others may feel they are good Christians because of all they do for the Lord and His church.

Some of those motives are acceptable to a point, but all are flawed in one critical way. Do you see how they all somehow turn back on oneself? If you serve for any of those reasons alone, you are serving for selfish motives. A true Christian teacher has a higher motive for teaching—a deep love for the Lord and a desire to please Him. He teaches because he cares about his students and wants to help them grow toward maturity in Christ. He knows that if his heart is not really in what he is doing or his motives are not right, his students will sense that and not respond to divine truth as they should.

## The Teacher's Devotional Life

A teacher who would present God's Word effectively and with power must first maintain a devotional life of fellowship with God. A real danger for Christian teachers is feeling that they are adequately maintaining their personal devotional lives by going through the routine of lesson study. Some may feel that because they spend considerable time each week in lesson preparation, additional Bible study is unnecessary. Although lesson study is of great benefit to the teacher's spiritual life, it does not take the place of maintaining a personal devotional life. This may be done in various ways, but of primary importance are Bible reading, prayer, devotional reading, and faithful church attendance.

## PERSONAL BIBLE STUDY

Guarding against taking a strictly analytical, academic approach to regular lesson study may enhance your devotional life. Learn to let the Scriptures speak to you first as a student, a seeker, then as a teacher. Try to find in the Bible passage or story the principles God has placed there for your personal growth.

Take a different approach to personal Bible study than you would to lesson preparation. Occasionally use a topical, word, historical, or biographical study method. Such techniques will necessitate the use of Bible study helps such as dictionaries, commentaries, and concordances. Using different translations and paraphrases will also add variety. Some of the new parallel texts are excellent for comparing different versions of the Bible.

Keep paper and a pencil handy and develop the habit of writing your reactions to what you read. Outline or diagram the passage or chapter. Underline key words and verses. Make up a personal commentary as you read, or write a paraphrase of the passage, putting the meaning of each verse into your own words. Keep your notes for future reference.

## PRAYER

Sunday school teachers experience the same prayer problems common to all believers: praying in generalities, having limited prayer concerns, getting into a rut. When praying for your class, try using a notebook with a page devoted to each student. List specific prayer needs, including the student's family. Page through the notebook as you pray. Be sure to record answers to prayer and give thanks.

Another way to keep your prayers specific and to avoid repetition is to pray for different needs on different days of the week. The following pattern is easy to remember because the prayer needs begin with the same letter as the days of the week:

> Monday—Missionaries
> Tuesday—Thanksgiving for answers
> Wednesday—Workers, pastors
> Thursday—Tasks, your work for the Lord
> Friday—Family, loved ones
> Saturday—Services, church ministries
> Sunday—Saints, fellow believers

In addition to spontaneous, extemporaneous prayer, occasionally use other prayer forms, such as prayers you have written, prayers written by others, prayer songs and choruses, prayer poetry, prayers from the Bible, and silent prayer.

One of the greatest hindrances to an effective devotional life is the problem of time. Consider some alternative times for devotions, such as early in the morning (dress first so you'll be fully awake), midmorning after the family leaves for school and work, at work or school during a break period or study hall, immediately after school or work, or immediately after the evening meal. You may find that you have to use different times on different days, depending on your personal or family schedule. Having a specific place for your devotions, preferably away from the day's normal activities, will also be helpful. Keep your Bible, prayer notebook, and other reading materials in that special place so you don't have to look for them each time.

## DEVOTIONAL READING

"Give me a worker who reads," leaders in every field cry. All leaders desire staff members who seize every opportunity to improve themselves in their field. Sunday school teachers should be such staff members. Reading offers numerous opportunities for spiritual and professional growth and development. It also imparts a keen awareness of the world in which you and your students live. Through the written word, you can associate with the great minds of the ages.

Lack of time to read is a common lament among teachers. The solution is to take advantage of even the briefest moments of available time. Get in the habit of carrying a small book in your purse or pocket. Did you know that a person who reads at normal speed for only 15 minutes each day will read 18 books in 1 year? As you read, use a pencil or highlighter to mark pertinent passages and make notes in the margins.

CHURCH ATTENDANCE

In Hebrews 10:25, Christians are told to be consistent in meeting with fellow believers. That admonition includes Sunday school teachers. Some teachers may feel exempt from attending church services and midweek Bible studies because they spend time in lesson preparation, not to mention periodic staff and training sessions. That, however, should not be the case for several reasons.

1. As a teacher you are constantly giving out to others; you need time to recharge your spiritual batteries. Church services give you that opportunity.

2. Because you are a role model to your students you need to be present at the services. Regardless of how much a pastor may urge his people to attend the services, they will not do so if you, their teacher, are not there.

3. If you do not attend the services, you will miss important opportunities to minister to students who respond to an altar call, express a prayer need, or linger to pray or talk with someone. As their teacher, you should be the first to reach out at such times. Undoubtedly you would be more than happy to do so, but you cannot if you are not there.

SOME QUESTIONS TO THINK ABOUT

Answering the questions below will help you evaluate your devotional life.

1. Do I experience daily fellowship with God in prayer and Bible reading?

2. Do I let the Bible lesson speak to me first as a learner before I approach it as a teacher?
3. Do I use a variety of resources to enrich my personal Bible study?
4. Do I focus my prayers on specific needs and situations?
5. Do I use different ways to express my thoughts and feelings to God in prayer?
6. Do I read from a variety of resources to enrich my spiritual life?
7. Do I take advantage of the brief moments of time available to read?
8. Do I serve as a good role model to my students in attending church services?

### Your Most Valuable Resource

What do you consider your most valuable asset or resource as a Sunday school teacher? Is it your knowledge of the Bible? your use of creative teaching methods? the effort you put into lesson preparation? your relationship with your students? Let's not have some immodest soul respond, "All of the above."

All those would certainly be valuable assets, but one resource is more important, more valuable, than any of them. It enables you to make effective use of all the others: time. Your use of time determines how well you know your Bible, how creatively you prepare your lessons, what methods you will be able to use, and how well you relate to your students.

Time is something a teacher never seems to have enough of. Actually, it's not the amount of time you have that determines your effectiveness, but what you do with what you have. Priorities come into focus at this point, for you will always have time to do what you really want to do. You may have housework, homework, or yard work to do, but if a friend calls with a more interesting proposal, you can usually find a way to get out of what you *need* to do, so you can do what you *want* to do, right? Setting priorities and making the most of your time will make you a better Sunday school teacher. The following ideas may help:

1. *Develop a to-do list.* Sometimes just listing things on paper can help you get better focused and organized. Items on your list may include reading the teachers quarterly, preparing the visual aids, writing your lesson outline, calling or writing last week's absentees, or making student assignments.

2. *Prioritize your list.* Circle two or three items you feel must be done first and concentrate on them. You may not get everything done, but at least you will know you are accomplishing the most important. Crossing off each item when you have completed it will motivate you to tackle the other items on your list.

3. *Set deadlines.* Most of us work better under pressure, so establish specific time limits for the tasks at hand. Accountability is also an important motivation. Share deadlines with a family member or friend who will agree to check up on you occasionally.

4. *Establish a weekly study routine.* Because we are all creatures of habit, most of us function better if we establish some kind of routine or pattern. However, some days or weeks may refuse to fit the pattern, so don't get too upset if things don't go according to your plan. But don't throw out the plan too hastily. Get back to the routine as quickly as you can and stick with it.

## A Matter of Attitude

Much of your effectiveness as a teacher will be determined by your attitude, how you approach your task. The following simple ideas can help you have the right attitude toward your work and make you a better teacher:

1. *Look for better ways to do the job.* There is room for improvement in any job, including teaching. Don't be satisfied with the status quo (Latin for "the mess we're in"). Just because "we've always done it that way" is no reason to continue doing

it that way. Be willing to try new ideas and approaches. Think of ways to cut corners without compromising quality. Open your heart and mind to the Holy Spirit, who is always fresh and creative.

2. *Find out what your job entails.* If you are a new worker, or your job involves new procedures, learn your duties quickly. Don't be afraid to ask questions. Talk to your predecessor, your fellow teachers, and your leaders. Study the handbook, policy manual, and job description. Ask the Lord to quicken your mind to learn.

3. *Do your share.* You can perform your job with a minimum of effort or you can pitch in and do your share. There is always more work than workers, so look for things to do without having to be asked. You needn't become a workaholic, but you can lend a helping hand and go the extra mile sometimes.

4. *Make an effort, not an excuse.* Human nature is such that we can find an excuse for nearly any undesirable action on our part. Don't excuse your failings; ask the Lord to help you overcome them. Remember, one day your work will be judged by the Master and rewarded as gold, silver, and precious stones, or rejected as wood, hay, and stubble.

5. *Develop a cheerful, cooperative spirit.* Remember how you do your job is primarily a matter of attitude, how you feel about it. If you make an effort, you *can* control your attitude. Work at being positive and keep your sense of humor. Being cheerful, however, is not the same as being frivolous; you should take your job seriously. Sunday school work is important business. Eternal destinies are at stake. The Holy Spirit can help you realize the importance of your task of reaching and teaching. Ask the Lord to give you a deep love and appreciation for your students, your fellow teachers, and your leaders. Thank Him also for the opportunity to serve Him through the Sunday school's ministries. The following adaptation of a poem by Edgar Guest sums up this chapter very well:[3]

### I'd Rather Watch a Teacher

I'd rather watch a teacher than hear one any day;

I'd rather have one walk with me than merely show the
way.
The eye's a better pupil and more willing than the ear;
Fine counsel is confusing, but example's always clear.
And the best of all the teachers are the ones who live their
creeds;
For to see God's truth in action is what everybody needs.
I can soon learn how to do it if you'll let me see it done.
I can watch your life in action, but your tongue too fast
may run.
And the lectures you deliver may be very wise and true;
But I'd rather get my lessons by observing what you do.
For I may misunderstand you and the high advice you
give;
But there's no misunderstanding how you act and how you
live.
I'd rather watch a teacher than hear one any day!

Once you understand what is required of you in your personal
life, you're ready to learn what is expected of you in the classroom. You'll find yourself wearing many different hats as you
fulfill your ministry as a Bible teacher.

## For Further Study

1. Why does God put a premium on being versus doing?
2. What should be the order of your commitments?
3. What should be your highest motive for teaching?
4. Why is it important that a teacher maintain a personal
   devotional life?
5. What are some practical ways to make more effective use
   of your time?
6. What attitudes do you need to work on to be a better teacher?

### NOTES

[1]Findley B. Edge, *Teaching for Results* (Nashville, Tenn.: Broadman Press,
1956), 223.

[2]Lawrence O. Richards, *You, the Teacher* (Chicago, Ill.: Moody Press, 1972), 49,50.

[3]Adapted from Edgar Guest's poem "Sermons We See," in *10 Seeds of Greatness,* by Denis Waitley (Old Tappan, N.J.: Fleming H. Revell Company, 1983), 209.

# 3
# The Professional Life of the Teacher

As a Sunday school teacher, you wear many hats and fulfill many roles. You're expected to be a classroom leader, communicator, and counselor, and a guide for the teaching-learning process. Success in any one of these roles would be a major accomplishment, but you're required to succeed in them all to make a difference in your students' lives. Teaching is quite a ministry, isn't it? Let's look in more detail at your many roles.

## Your Role as a Group Leader

The group is the basic working unit in Christian education. As teachers and leaders, we find ourselves continually involved with people in group settings, both inside and outside the classroom. To be effective as a group leader, we must understand how people function within groups, what factors hinder the group process, and how to structure and direct positive group activities.

### GROUP ROLES

Individual members carry out various roles or functions within the group. Being aware of these roles may help you understand the students who make up your class. Some members play positive roles: the *harmonizer* seeks to reconcile opposing positions; the *clarifier* restates issues for solution and tries to clarify what the group has agreed on; the *explorer* suggests alternative procedures or solutions and leads the group in searching for answers; the *catalyst* seeks to involve other students in discussions or class activities; the *tension-reducer* jokes or clowns at appropriate times to help release tensions; and the *programmer* leads the group in planning practical action.

Unfortunately some class members may play negative roles: the *dominator* offers long monologues or is authoritative or overly dogmatic; the *belittler* minimizes the potential of the group and the contributions of others; the *manipulator* tries to manage the group to accomplish his predetermined agenda; the *bandwagon-jumper* senses the drift of a discussion and always takes the popular side; the *dodger* makes sudden shifts in position to avoid taking a stand on issues; the *scapegoater* pins blame and responsibility on someone or something as an outlet for personal frustration; the *sulker* expresses resentment toward the group or toward particular members; and the *devil's advocate* always takes an opposing position just for the sake of argument and is usually more devil than advocate.

Your responsibility as a leader is to identify these group roles, learn how to utilize the positive people, and not allow the negative ones to deter the class' progress.

FACTORS HINDERING THE GROUP PROCESS

To be effective in leading and teaching, we need to understand some of the factors that can hinder the group learning process.

1. *Conflict*—Many situations can cause conflict in a group: members vying for status or position, members perceiving that some students are class favorites, or discipline and order not being maintained. Conflict usually surfaces as a symptom of more serious underlying problems. The wise leader looks beyond the obvious situation to the root cause.

2. *The hidden agenda*—Some class members may focus on matters that are not out in the open, such as personal problems, for which they seek answers. Others may come to class with hip-pocket solutions, waiting for an opportune moment to in-

troduce their ideas. Little group progress is made until these hidden agenda items are identified and dealt with, whether inside or outside the classroom.

3. *Indecision*—The group process is hindered when indecisiveness reigns or when discussions stall over insignificant details. When members feel little or no progress is being made, they may become overassertive or simply withdraw from the group, either psychologically or physically.

4. *Apathy*—Indifference to the group, lack of enthusiasm, poor participation, frequent absenteeism, reluctance to accept responsibility, and failure to carry out assignments are indications of group apathy. Sometimes the problem lies within the individual; sometimes its cause can be found in the way the group functions. In either case, you are responsible to discover the reason(s) and take corrective action.

CREATING A GROUP ATMOSPHERE AND DIRECTING ACTIVITIES

An important part of your role as a leader is to create a warm, cooperative group atmosphere. The following suggestions will help you to do so:

1. Rearrange the seating to create a more informal setting— a semicircle or around tables. Also dispense with all unnecessary formalities, such as raising hands, standing to speak, using titles, and other classroom rituals.

2. Encourage individuals to express their feelings openly and honestly. Listen carefully and accurately restate the student's comments. Show appreciation for all ideas expressed.

3. Help the group accept new members and new ideas with a minimum of conflict. See that all sides of an issue are fairly represented and help the class integrate new ideas into common group purposes. Avoid pushing students to participate before they are ready, which puts them on the spot.

You can do much to direct learning activities.

1. Help the group determine goals and objectives.

2. Identify the students' resources.
3. Help the students participate in meaningful ways.
4. Work with the students; don't do things for them.
5. Help evaluate the group's progress.

## Your Role as a Communicator

As a Christian teacher, you are in the communications business. In fact, communication is at the center of all the church's teaching ministries. However, in spite of its importance, we have not always paid much attention to studying the communications process. Often we have assumed we understand each other simply because we share a common belief and experience.

### UNDERSTANDING COMMUNICATION

Anyone with the desire can learn the skill of effective communication. First, however, you have to understand it. The dictionary defines communication as a process of transmitting a verbal or written message, or as an exchange of information between individuals. That sounds simple enough until you realize there are at least six versions of every communicated message: (1) what the speaker intended to say; (2) what the speaker actually said; (3) what the speaker thinks he said; (4) what the listener wanted to hear; (5) what the listener actually heard; and (6) what the listener thinks he heard.

The following are important aspects to remember regarding communication:

1. Communication is a two-way process. It involves both sending and receiving a message.
2. Communication involves both exchanging feelings and exchanging ideas.
3. Communication involves effort. It doesn't just happen. It results from using basic communication skills.

Communication involves the following eight steps or elements:

1. The sender forms a message in his mind.
2. The sender sends the message to the receiver verbally, on paper, or in another form.
3. The receiver hears the content of the message.
4. The receiver assigns meaning to the message.
5. The receiver forms a response in his mind.
6. The receiver responds with feedback to the original speaker.
7. The original speaker hears the content of the second message.
8. The original speaker assigns meaning to the message.

Experience, perceived intentions, the hearer's needs, the setting in which the message is exchanged, and the speaker's and hearer's feelings and self-image all affect the communications process at various points.

Communication can be either verbal or nonverbal. Verbal communication includes sounds, music, spoken words, or a written message. Accent and voice inflection may also be considered part of verbal communication. Nonverbal communication includes appearance, voice, facial expressions, gestures, body language, spatial relations, or any other physical behavior.

The largest part of communication often does not involve words at all. By some estimates as much as 93 percent of the message's total impact reaches the recipient by nonverbal means, including 38 percent by tone of voice.

REMOVING THE BARRIERS

Barriers often hinder communication at various points.

1. *Barriers within the speaker*—A negative self-image dramatically affects our ability to communicate. Lack of self-confidence will be reflected in unspoken questions such as, Are my ideas wanted here? Are they worth expressing? Are others really interested in what I have to say? Inadequate preparation also affects the teacher's ability to communicate.

A discrepancy between words and deeds may also be a barrier

to communication. Your actions may speak so loudly that your listeners cannot hear what you are saying. Students have difficulty believing a message that is not reflected in the teacher's life.

2. *Barriers between the speaker and the listeners*—Such barriers may include physical obstacles, such as noise, distractions, interruptions, an inability to see or hear, or physical discomfort. Language and jargon may also be barriers. No two people receive an identical meaning from the same words because they do not have identical experiences. One study revealed the 500 most commonly used words in the English language produce a total of 11,500 different meanings, or an average of 23 different meanings per word.[1]

3. *Barriers within the listener*—Every listener sees and hears a combination of what is outside him and what is in his head and heart. In other words, who the listener is determines what he hears. It's called selective perception. One hears what he wants to hear, paying attention only to what interests him.[2]

Another factor complicating the communications process is that we can listen at least five times faster than we normally speak. "Most speakers in conversation utter somewhere between 120 and 180 words per minute."[3] With compressed speech, an individual can comprehend up to 500 words per minute. Speed readers comprehend thousands of words per minute. This time differential allows the listener's mind to wander and plan his response.

4. *Barriers of time and space*—Bible culture was far different from our modern culture. We do things quite differently today. While we believe the Bible still speaks to us today, our challenge as Christian teachers is to find ways to make its message clear and relevant.

IMPROVING CLASSROOM COMMUNICATION

So what can you do to improve the effectiveness of your classroom communication? The following basic principles will help:

1. **Remove physical barriers.** Do all you can to eliminate

distractions and interruptions. Arrange the seating to direct attention away from anything that could detract from the learning process. Make it possible for every student to see and hear clearly. Help the group to be physically comfortable. Monitor the temperature and air quality.

2. Clarify and simplify ideas before presenting them. Someone has said, "Think deeply, but speak simply." Use a variety of illustrations to help clarify meanings. When you present abstract ideas, try to use concrete words and examples, especially with young children.

3. Work for two-way communication. Use participative learning methods such as buzz groups, panels, writing, art, and drama. The best way to encourage participation is to use a variety of informational, rhetorical, and thought-provoking questions. In this way you shift the focus and responsibility from the teacher to the students, causing them to feel a part of the communications process.

4. Use audiovisuals to emphasize and clarify your message. Retention is as much as six times greater when teaching is reinforced by instructional media. Audiovisuals also provide opportunity for student involvement and participation.

5. Plan your lesson introduction carefully. Begin with something that has built-in interest for your students. Help the group see where you are going and how you will get there.

6. Use variety in your presentation. Plan to use at least three or four different methods or techniques in a teaching session. Look for ways to repeat concepts that are new to the group. Summarize your presentation to reinforce main ideas. Teach to communicate your message, not to impress your students.

IMPROVING PERSONAL COMMUNICATION

To improve your personal effectiveness as a communicator try working on some of the following:

1. Strive to develop a nonjudgmental attitude. Smile, be friendly. Call the students by name. Get to know them personally. Express appreciation for the ideas they share with the

class. Watch for others who may want to contribute and ensure that they are heard.

2. Learn to be a good listener. Seek not only to be understood, but also to understand. Concentrate on what is said, not on what you will reply. Use appropriate body language to demonstrate interest: lean forward, look the person in the eye, nod your head. Ask questions to clarify ideas. Look for opportunities to train your students to be better listeners. They will benefit from that skill throughout their lives.

3. Be positive in your relationships. Give praise and commendation whenever possible, but be sincere. Point out the students' strengths and abilities.

4. Accept your students as they are. Get to know them and love them as real people, and let them get to know you as a real person. Provide opportunities for contact outside the classroom.

## Your Role as a Counselor

Not all of your teaching will focus on the students as a group. Some of your most effective ministry will be in one-on-one counseling situations. As a teacher, you will often be the first counselor your students seek for help. While you may not feel qualified as a counselor in the professional sense, you can still have an effective ministry. In fact, many Christian psychologists believe trained lay persons can be very effective as counselors.[4] That is not to say professional counseling is unnecessary, but many student counseling needs can be met by a concerned Christian teacher. At the same time, the teacher should be wise enough to realize when he is not qualified to handle a situation, and he should refer the student to the pastor or a professional counselor.

COUNSELING OPPORTUNITIES

When you are aware of your students' needs, numerous counseling opportunities will present themselves. Before class, talk to those who arrive early. Be alert to those who linger after class. Perhaps they have something important they want to share. The altar time is another excellent opportunity to counsel and pray with your students.

Casual meetings with your students outside the church provide further opportunities. You must go where your students are—to their neighborhood, their school activities, their workplace, shopping areas, or other regular locations. Be friendly and open. Plan to visit your students in their homes at least once a year. Five minutes there can tell you more about them than a year in the classroom. When you visit younger students, spend time with them, not just with their parents.

You may want to consider setting up a teacher-student conference plan for your class. You will first need to check with both the leaders and the parents. Factors to consider include schedules, meeting places, transportation, referral of problem cases, and other special circumstances.

QUALITIES OF A GOOD COUNSELOR

Students look for and appreciate the following qualities in the teacher who desires to be an effective counselor:

1. *Be trustworthy.* A good counselor must be able to keep confidences. Someone has said, "The heart of a counselor is like a graveyard—many problems lie buried there." Resist the temptation to use situations learned in personal counseling as lesson illustrations, even if you change the names to protect the innocent. If a student recognizes himself in the illustration, no matter how many details are altered, he will be convinced that many others in the class recognize him too.

2. *Be available.* As a good counselor, be willing to take time to help. You must be there when your students want to talk. At the same time, do not push yourself on them. They must come to you.

3. *Be a good listener.* It is impossible to listen if you do all the talking. Concentrate on what is said, not on your reply. Ask questions that will get to the bottom of the matter, and try not to be shocked at what you hear.

4. *Be genuine.* Your students, young and old alike, will recognize the real thing when they see it. Demonstrate an understanding, patient attitude as you express compassion and love. Let your students know you are trying to understand how they feel. You must put yourself in their shoes while avoiding emotional involvement.

5. *Be accepting.* You must love and accept the student as he is, not as you would like him to be. You need not condone what he is doing, but you must not reject him as a person. You must be his friend not his judge.

6. *Be alert.* Students who need counseling will not always seek help. Sometimes their silence will be a cry for help. Therefore, a good counseling teacher will cultivate a spiritual sensitivity, detect the need for help, and, if necessary, initiate the counseling situation.

7. *Be consistent.* Your own life must be firmly rooted in God's Word as you demonstrate spiritual growth. To inspire confidence in your students, you must demonstrate stability and emotional maturity. To remain credible, you must practice what you preach.

8. *Be relevant.* Don't preach to your students, especially the "when I was your age" sermon. Avoid trying to apply your personal solutions to their problems. Don't be too quick to say, "I understand," unless you know you really do. Don't make decisions for a student that he should make for himself.

9. *Be patient.* Avoid premature judgments and hasty conclusions. Make your counseling a process, not an event. Take time to explore, understand, and resolve the problem. Sound conclusions cannot be forced. They must be allowed to emerge.

10. *Be effective.* Use the Bible in counseling. Don't hesitate to show what the Bible says concerning the matter. At the same time, do not offer overly simplistic answers to complicated problems. If you don't have a good answer, don't make up one.

## Your Role as an Encourager

Cindy comes into the primary classroom with tears in her

eyes. Her parents just had another big argument on the way to church. She's afraid they don't like each other anymore. She needs a word of encouragement.

Kevin, a 15-year-old, comes to class on Sunday after getting cut from the track team last Friday. It's the only team he will ever have a chance to make. He also needs a word of encouragement.

All around you—at home, school, work, and church—people feel discouraged and defeated. They wonder if anyone knows how deeply they hurt, and if anyone, including God, really cares. They come into your classroom looking for encouragement.

What they don't need is someone to add to their woes with an unintentional, but flippant remark like, "Oh, don't look so glum." Or, "Cheer up, things could be worse." Such remarks convey the message that Christians shouldn't become discouraged or depressed.

William Barclay, a well-known Bible scholar, maintains that encouragement is one of man's highest duties. He points out that it takes little effort to laugh at ideas, pour cold water on enthusiasm, and otherwise spread discouragement. The world is filled with discouragers; Christians have a duty to be encouragers. Barclay advises that when we encounter a person who is struggling, we should extend a compliment, a sincere thank-you, or a note of appreciation. That may be all that is needed to help the person stand. We too will be blessed when we speak an encouraging word.

As a Christian teacher, you are in the best position to offer a word of encouragement. You probably know your students better than anyone else in the church. Your words may mean more than those of an acquaintance. Consider the following ways to fulfill your role as an encourager:

1. Remind your students often that they are special in God's sight. He made them just the way they are for a specific reason. He watches over them and is working in their lives (Psalm 139; Ephesians 2:10; Philippians 1:6). When your students see they

are special to you, the truths of these verses will be even more meaningful to them.

2. Cultivate an appreciative attitude. Look for opportunities to offer sincere praise and commendation. Seek out specific things to admire in others. Take advantage of every chance to affirm your students. Don't overlook simple things such as a warm smile or a firm handshake.

3. Avoid flippant remarks or easy answers. Telling a student to go pray about a problem may indeed bring the answer he needs, but that is not always enough. James says we must do more than say, "Be . . . warmed and filled" (James 2:16). We must be willing to become involved in our students' lives and to spend time helping them solve their problems.

Learn to be a Barnabas, whose name means "a son of encouragement." Your students will love you for it, and you will see the difference it makes in their lives.

## For Further Study

1. What different group roles do you see your students performing?
2. What can you do to create a more accepting classroom atmosphere?
3. What is your personal definition of the communications process?
4. What barriers are hindering communication? What can you do to remove them?
5. What opportunities do you have to function as a counselor?
6. What do you think is the most important quality for a Christian counselor?

### NOTES

[1]Olan Hendrix, *Management for the Christian Worker* (Santa Barbara, Calif.: Quill Publications, 1976), 100.

[2]H. Norman Wright, *So You're Getting Married* (Ventura, Calif.: Regal Books, 1985), 159.

[3]R. R. Allen, S. Anderson, and others, *Speech in American Society* (Columbus, Ohio: Charles E. Merrill Publishing Co., 1968), 138.

[4]Gary Collins, *How To Be a People Helper* (Ventura, Calif.: Vision House, 1976), 12,13.

# 4

# The Place of the Student in Bible Teaching

As a Christian teacher, you work with two large bodies of information, the Bible and related lesson materials, and your students' characteristics and needs. A thorough knowledge of both areas is essential for successful teaching. The situation can be diagrammed as follows:

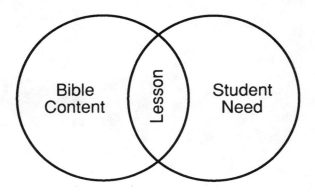

A class session contains Bible content that is not a part of the lesson. Likewise, some of the student's needs are not met in the session. The area in which Bible content overlaps with the student's needs and interests is where the lesson develops. That means to be effective, you must know and understand your students—how they learn, what interests and motivates them, and how to involve them in the learning experience. This chapter will address those topics.

## Understanding Your Students

Because the students are at the core of the teaching-learning process, studying them as a group and as individuals is essential. Learn the physical, mental, emotional, social, psychological, and spiritual characteristics of the age-group you teach. Those traits form a composite of the typical student. Of course, no student will conform to them in every way. Some of the characteristics will be spelled out in more detail in chapters 8 and 9.

Always remember you are not merely teaching a class; you are teaching one-of-a-kind individuals, each unique in many ways. In his book *How To Get Along With People in the Church,* A. Donald Bell suggests the following 10 ways to get to know your students as individuals:

1. Be open-minded. Avoid forming snap judgments.
2. Study any available records the church may have.
3. Make the most of listening opportunities.
4. Avoid comparing the students with others.
5. Visit the students' homes.
6. Try to see the students in different situations.
7. Study the students' friends.
8. Learn what interests the students.
9. Find out what occupies the students' leisure time.
10. Find out what motivates the students.[1]

### WHAT YOU SHOULD KNOW

Knowing something about each student's family will help explain the student's attitudes or behaviors in the classroom. Learn how many children are in the family; where the student fits in the birth order; what kind of relationship exists between the parents and the child; how the child is disciplined; and whether he is part of a single-parent, two-parent, or blended family. Knowing if the home provides supplemental Christian training will also be helpful. Can you call on the parents to help their child study the lesson or learn the memory work?

Also learn something about the student's church background. Is he a member? Does he attend regularly? What is his doctrinal heritage? What other church activities is he involved in? Are his close friends from inside or outside the church?

Other questions to answer include, Has the student accepted Christ as his Savior? Is he growing in his Christian experience? Has he been baptized in water? Has he received the infilling of the Holy Spirit? Is he sharing his faith? Has he established a daily time of Bible reading and prayer? Is he struggling with any spiritual problems?

If you teach school-age children or youth, you should know what grade each student is in and where he attends school. If a student is having difficulty understanding the material or seems to be unchallenged, the explanation may lie in knowing how he is doing in school. With teens it is important to know the student's extracurricular involvements. With adults it helps to know the student's educational background. How far did he go in school? What degrees does he have? What special training has he received? Is he involved in any continuing education programs?

Career goals, vocational interests, and current job status are important information when teaching teenagers. Knowing where each adult works, his hours, the length of his present employment, the special skills required in his job, and whether he is happy in his work can help you minister more effectively. Knowing the job interests and skills of your retired students will help you discover valuable ministries the students could participate in, both in your class and in the church.

A few other personal things you should know about your students are their birthdays, nicknames, hobbies, favorite leisure activities, community involvements, leadership skills, and experience.

How You Can Know This

A personal questionnaire may be the easiest way to gather

facts. More subjective information can be obtained by visiting the student's home, neighborhood, school, or place of employment. Visiting a student's schoolteacher may also prove helpful and will demonstrate that your church joins the school in taking a personal interest in each student. Because teachers are usually observant of students both inside and outside the classroom, they can be good sources of information.

Scheduling a conference with each student sometime near the beginning of the school year may be helpful with teens and adults. Such sessions provide an opportunity to engage the student in conversation, to determine his spiritual progress and felt needs, and to offer personal counseling as needed.

WHAT TO DO WITH WHAT YOU KNOW

The information and understanding you gather about your students should be arranged in a usable format. One idea is to compile a notebook with a page or two for each student containing factual data, your impressions of his educational and spiritual development, and perhaps interesting anecdotes from the class. Such information about your students would be a boon in planning lessons to meet their real needs and in helping them to solve personal problems. You can also use the notebook as a prayer log. Consult it before visiting a student or his family. When the student moves on to another class, some of the information can be passed on to the next teacher.

## Understanding How Your Students Learn

Henrietta Mears, the great Christian education pioneer, is widely credited with saying, "The teacher has not taught until the pupil has learned." In other words, to be effective as a Christian teacher, you must understand how your students learn and teach them accordingly. Teaching this way is sometimes called the "guided learning process" and is basically a matter of guiding student activity so the desired learning takes place.

Because you know their interests, needs, and abilities, you

can help the students to discover biblical truths for themselves and guide them to make personal applications. Supply direction and resources to bring about the desired response, but never do anything for your students that they can more profitably do themselves.

This approach to teaching is like conducting a guided tour. The competent guide is familiar with all the points of interest so he can help the group map out their itinerary and answer their questions. He makes the necessary arrangements and leads the group to the main attractions. The tourists receive firsthand experience with new people and new places. You function as a guide of the learning process in several important ways.

## GUIDING THE INTERESTS OF THE STUDENTS

Students learn best when they are ready to learn. Starting the learning process with their needs and interests in focus is the way to foster that readiness. Gain your students' attention and start with their felt needs. To do this you must know where your students are in their knowledge and understanding of spiritual truth and teach accordingly. Helping the students to look for answers to their questions or problems will prepare them to receive Bible truth.

Students also learn more readily when they see the relationship of the parts to the whole. Preview a new series of lessons with your students and periodically review past lessons to keep them in focus. Posters and pictures can aid in the process. Occasionally assign several students to recap past lessons.

## GUIDING SENSORIAL EXPERIENCES

We all learn through our five senses, the gateways to our mind. Students learn best through a variety of sensorial experiences. The following statistics make that clear:

## STUDENTS RETAIN UP TO ...

10 percent of what they hear.
30 percent of what they see.
50 percent of what they see and hear.
70 percent of what they see, hear, and say.
90 percent of what they see, hear, say, and do.

## ABILITY TO RECALL

| Method of Teaching | Recall—3 Hours | Recall—3 Days |
|---|---|---|
| Hearing alone | 70 percent | 10 percent |
| Seeing alone | 72 percent | 20 percent |
| Hearing and seeing | 85 percent | 65 percent |

The obvious conclusion: learning is more effective and lasting when it involves several senses. Your role, then, is to use a variety of teaching methods that appeal to multiple senses.

### GUIDING THE LEARNING ACTIVITIES OF THE STUDENTS

Students learn best through activity because learning is an active, not a passive, experience. Learning does not happen to the students; it is something they do. As the figures above reveal, the higher the level of involvement, the more effective and long-lasting the learning will be.

The secret to good teaching is to guide the students in the same process of Bible study you engaged in to prepare the lesson. You cannot predigest all the material and present it in neat, premeasured doses to the students. Instead, you must constantly strive to involve them in Bible study for themselves.

Begin by deciding what part of the Bible story or Scripture passage you will cover. A well-stated lesson aim focusing on an active response will guide you in the selection process.

You must also choose the teaching methods that will best accomplish your objectives and decide what additional materials you will use. Students learn vicariously, or indirectly, through stories, illustrations, and examples. Their feelings can be aroused, their emotions stirred, and their imagination activated. Students learn directly through their involvement in activities such as projects, assignments, handcrafts, discussions, dramas, and roleplays. The best methods actively involve the students, appeal to their interests and needs, and reinforce learning.

## GUIDING THE MOTIVATION OF THE STUDENTS

Your task as a teacher is to win the attention of the inattentive, to interest the disinterested, and to awaken the unconcerned. To do this you must be a motivator, inspiring your students to attend regularly, to study, to become involved, and to respond to the truths of the Word. Because motivation is the cause of learning, it is obviously a crucial factor in the teaching-learning process. It activates, sustains, and directs learning. One of your primary tasks, then, is to motivate your students to learn, and students are best motivated when learning is made desirable, rewarding, exciting, and fun.

### Types of Motivation

The two types of motivation in the teaching-learning process are *extrinsic* and *intrinsic*. Extrinsic motivation, as the word implies, is stimulation that is external to the learning experience, such as prizes, awards, games, and contests. Intrinsic motivation results from the satisfaction of the learner's inner needs. The student's personal desires, drives, and interests are involved.

There has been a great deal of debate on the merits of both types of motivation. Each has its place. Intrinsic motivation seems to be more in keeping with the goals of Christian education. It seeks to make the study of the Word so significant and meaningful that the learner receives genuine satisfaction. The gospel, in itself, is the best possible motivation. It makes a difference in people's lives. Learning is enhanced when the students see how their needs are met through the application of biblical principles to their lives.

On the other hand, extrinsic motivation is beneficial when used wisely. The danger comes in extreme and exclusive use of such motivation. In appealing to external motivation, you must evaluate not only its immediate results, but also what attitudes, emotions, and possible conflicts it may produce. Another problem with extrinsic motivation is that you must continually increase the size of the reward.

### Factors Generating Motivation

1. A sense of acceptance and belonging—Work to build a group spirit in the class.
2. An atmosphere of love and concern—Genuinely love your students and take an interest in their lives and spiritual growth.
3. A sense of achievement—Give your students individual attention to ensure that their activities will be successful.
4. A challenge—Help your students set high goals for themselves. Give them assignments, and follow up to see that they complete them. Let your students know you expect something from them.
5. Involvement—Let your students suggest learning goals to strive for and ways to achieve them. Let your students share in planning class activities, projects, and courses of study.
6. A real-life application—Make an effort to learn about the daily situations your students face, and focus your teaching on their needs.

### GUIDING THE QUALITY OF STUDENT RELATIONSHIPS

Students learn best when they have a sense of belonging and a feeling of participation and involvement in the class. As an effective teacher, you can guide the development of class relationships by being a caring person. You must love your students not only as a group, but also as unique individuals facing personal problems and cherishing personal hopes and dreams. You must be interested not only in their spiritual needs, but also in every area of their lives. Someone has aptly paraphrased

1 Corinthians 13:13 to read, "As a teacher, I must possess these three—knowledge, technique, and love. But the greatest of these is love."

## Preparing Your Students To Learn

Understanding how learning occurs and getting it to happen are often two different things. The key to a successful teaching-learning experience is proper preparation for both the teacher and the students. As a teacher, you are encouraged and instructed in how to prepare your lessons, your visual aids, and your own heart. Of course, you need to do all these things, but you also need to know how to prepare your students to learn. Consider what can happen if you don't:

It's 5 minutes past starting time in the junior class at the Lots-O-Luck Sunday school. Although the juniors moved to the beginners classroom last month, the furnishings and decorations still have not been changed. Since the teacher hasn't yet arrived, the girls entertain themselves by drawing pictures on the chalkboard, while the boys build a pyramid of chairs on top of a table.

The teacher enters the room scowling and reprimands the students. After several minutes he gets the class settled down and asks, "Okay, class, what did we talk about last week?" His question is greeted with silence.

"Just what I thought. You weren't paying attention, were you? Well, this week we're studying the 13th chapter of Romans. Susie, you read verse 1. Bill, you read verse 2. Debbie, you read verse 3. . . ."

The students haltingly read the assigned verses, mispronouncing many of the more difficult words, to the delight of the rest of the class.

"Teacher, what does or-di-nance mean?" asks Bob.

"Oh, don't bother me with your silly questions, Bob. You're just trying to trick me. Besides, we're wasting time. I have to get through my lesson."

At that response the students sink back in their seats while the teacher drones on, lecturing about how awful it is the way people break the laws today. Finally the bell rings and the students make a mad dash for the door, ending another exciting day at the Lots-O-Luck Sunday school in Ye Old Boredom Factory.

The teacher failed to prepare his students for learning. You can easily spot the problems.

1. Lack of physical preparation—The furniture was the wrong size and the decorations were inappropriate.

2. Lack of mental preparation—The teacher did not try to gain the students' interest or meet their needs. He did nothing to stimulate thought or discussion. He had only one goal in mind, to get through his lesson.

3. Lack of emotional preparation—The teacher exhibited an unfriendly, critical, suspicious, disrespectful attitude and showed no interest in the students' questions. On top of that, he was late for class.

What's the solution? Adequate physical, mental, and emotional preparation is needed.

## PHYSICAL PREPARATION

Uncomfortable students will not be attentive learners. Your first responsibility, then, is to ensure the students' physical well-being. The room's general appearance is an important consideration. A neat, orderly room makes for more well-behaved students. A bright, cheery room with appropriate wall decorations enhances learning. More will be said about this in chapter 5.

## MENTAL PREPARATION

If you do not capture your students' attention in the opening moments, you may lose it for the entire period. Plan a good introduction to your lesson. Older children, youth, and adults enjoy a mental challenge, so use thought-provoking questions and discussions. Pose a problem and lead the class into the Scriptures to find the answers. Case studies and open-ended stories are great ways to get started. Also use assignments and other activities to stimulate mental preparation during the week.

## EMOTIONAL PREPARATION

All of us do best what we enjoy most. Prepare your students emotionally by making learning desirable, exciting, and fun. Your own attitude toward the learning experience will greatly affect your students' attitude.

Creating a relaxed atmosphere in which your students feel free to respond is essential. Having an open, accepting, honest attitude will elicit a like response from your students.

It is also important to accept your students as they are, for what they are, and to respect them as real people. Put yourself in their place and try to see things from their point of view.

Of course, the best thing you can do to prepare your students emotionally is to love them, to really care for them as individuals, in spite of how they may respond to you. Find ways to actively demonstrate your love for them not only in words and gestures, but also in actions and deeds.

## For Further Study

1. What are some things you can do to get to know your students better?
2. How can an understanding of your students' home and family life help you teach them more effectively?
3. How can information about your students be helpful in planning your lessons?
4. In what ways does the teacher function as a tour guide?
5. What are some ways you can involve your students in the learning process?

6. What can you do to motivate your students to be better learners?

## NOTES

[1]A. Donald Bell, *How To Get Along With People in the Church* (Grand Rapids, Mich.: Zondervan Publishing House, 1960), 59–64.

# 5

# The Plan for Effective Bible Teaching

Five minutes before the start of Sunday school, Fred is a busy man. In fact, some of his students are already arriving and would like to talk to him if he weren't so busy. But Fred has more important things to do than to talk to his students. He's frantically reading through his lesson manual circling key points to cover. He's also searching through his teaching aids packet for the suggested handouts. The room still has to be set up and the bulletin board changed.

When Fred finally gets started, he does most of the work—telling the story, looking up relevant verses, asking questions—while his students sit passively. Yes indeed, Fred is a busy man this morning.

Down the hall, a very different scene unfolds in Mark's classroom. Mark is busy too, but in a different way. He wrote his lesson plan early in the week. He prepared his teaching resources and placed them in order yesterday afternoon. And he set up the room and placed the handouts on the tables 30 minutes ago. As his students arrive, Mark asks them to look through magazines for pictures relating to the lesson's theme. A few of the students sit at a table and talk with him about their week while looking up verses to be used in the session. Once the class starts, Mark continues functioning in a relaxed way, guiding the activities.

Obviously, the two teachers planned and prepared their class sessions far differently. One began days in advance; the other waited until the last possible moment. One saw his role as a guide to the learning activities of his students, a role he could fulfill from behind the scenes. The other saw himself as the dispenser of information, a role requiring him to be the center of attention. The iceberg theory applies to an effective Bible teacher's planning and presentation efforts.

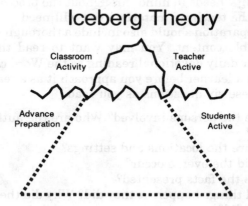

# Iceberg Theory

A good classroom teaching-learning experience is the result of much planning and preparation. The teacher is active in planning during the week so the students can be active learners in the classroom. How you function as a teacher is determined by how you plan and prepare. Let's consider some of the steps involved in the process and how they can make a difference in your teaching.

## Preliminary Planning

Lesson preparation should begin weeks in advance. Familiarize yourself with the entire series of lessons in the curriculum cycle, which your superintendent or Christian education director should have provided for you. If you have not received a copy of the curriculum cycle, you may request it directly from the publisher.

Start each new quarter by reading the entire teachers manual in one sitting. This will help you see how each lesson fits into the whole. Also read through the materials in the student quarterly to know what the students will be studying. As you prepare, make note of issues and questions that arise and jot down ideas for teaching methods, lesson illustrations, student assignments, and ways to introduce and apply the lessons. Keep your students' needs in mind throughout the process and begin collecting the teaching materials you will need.

Your preparation should also include a thorough study of the lesson's Bible content. You may want to read the passages during your daily devotional reading so the Word can speak to you first as a learner before you approach it as a teacher. Keep in mind these six questions as you read.

1. Who are the persons involved? Who are the author and the readers?
2. Where are the locations and settings?
3. When did the events occur?
4. How are the facts presented?
5. Why did things happen as they did? Why did the author say what he did?
6. What is the relevance of the story or passage to us today?

As you plan your lesson, read the passage or story in several Bible versions or paraphrases. Look up any unfamiliar words or ideas in a Bible dictionary, commentary, or handbook and study the context and historical setting.

## Planning Teaching-Learning Aims

An old country philosopher said, "The reason some folk don't git no whar is that they wun't goin' no whar in the fust place." The same could be said about many Christian teachers—their teaching is aimless. Too often the students learn little because the teacher is not sure what he wants the students to learn. The teacher is like the person in the rhyme who said,

"I shot an arrow into the air.
It fell to earth I know not where."

What did he expect? He started out without a target and ended up without an arrow.

Many teachers spend time studying the lesson, constructing a lesson plan, collecting teaching materials, and planning the use of methods, but they fail to have or to write a lesson aim to guide them. Communicating God's Word to meet the students' needs is too important to be left to aimless effort. If every teacher would devise a good lesson aim, that would improve the quality of Bible teaching in the local church more than anything else.

### DEFINING LESSON AIMS

The dictionary defines an aim as "activity directed in an orderly manner toward the realization of some end." In Bible teaching, the aim is simply a description of what the teacher wants to happen in the students' lives as a result of learning the lesson. Teaching aims cover a wide scope.

The *overall aim* is to produce growth toward maturity in Christ. Paul gives us this ultimate goal in Ephesians 4:13, "Until we all reach unity in the faith and in the knowledge of the Son of God and become mature, attaining to the whole measure of the fullness of Christ" (NIV). Although this goal may not be achieved in our earthly bodies, it is a lifelong goal for which we must always strive.

The overall goal will be achieved in part and then only through a series of shorter, intermediate aims. The teacher should state these intermediate aims as *quarterly and unit aims*. Formulating an aim for the entire series of lessons will help the teacher see how each lesson contributes to the whole. The quarterly aim should then be divided into several unit aims covering two or more lessons that seem to go together.

*Individual lesson aims* are the immediate steps taken to accomplish the unit and quarterly aims and, ultimately, they contribute to the overall objective itself. We will focus our attention in the rest of this section on structuring individual lesson aims.

Lesson aims are composed of three parts:

1. Knowledge, or a mastery of Bible content—This aim is usually stated, "To help my students to know . . .," or, "To help my students understand that . . . ." Most lesson aims, if written out at all, are of this type.
2. Attitudes, or a change of feelings and desires—This aim is usually stated, "To help my students feel . . .," or, "To help my students want to . . . ."
3. Actions, or a change in behavior—This aim is stated, "To help my students begin to . . . ."

A well-thought-out lesson aim will include a balance of those three parts. However, if the ultimate aim of Christian teaching is to see the students grow toward maturity in Christ, teaching with a content or knowledge aim alone, or with an aim focusing only on attitudes and desires, will be insufficient. To teach for growth, we must teach for a change in conduct. To *know* and to *feel* are part of the response to *do.* To be sure, a change in behavior is often preceded by a change in knowledge and attitude, but teaching for a change in conduct and behavior is the kind of effective Bible teaching that makes a real difference in lives.

## THE NEED FOR LESSON AIMS

Christian education's goal is to bring the learner to maturity in Christ. Each lesson should be a step in that direction—a change, a response bringing the learner closer to the goal of conformity to the image of Christ.

Before the teacher can plan for learning to take place, he must clearly know the end he desires to attain. Simply put, he must decide where he is going before he can plan how to get there. The clearer the aim, the easier it will be to plan for its attainment.

A lesson aim also keeps the teacher from trying to accomplish too much in a single session. Most Bible teaching is more like a shotgun blast than a well-aimed rifle shot. It may hit a wide area of spiritual needs, but often without enough impact to bring about a real change or to make a significant difference. The students leave with a few pellets of Bible truth embedded in them, but without enough to make much of a difference in how they think, feel, or act.

A teacher can improve results by focusing his lesson plans on a single area of need. A well-designed lesson aim will help him make a significant difference in the chosen area.

A good teaching aim is the major controlling factor in the teaching-learning process. All decisions are made on the basis of the stated aim. Methods and materials are included or discarded based on their relevance to the stated aim. A good aim also serves as a basis for evaluation. Did the methods you used help you to reach your goal? Did you include the right materials? Did you see a change in your students? Your aim can help answer these questions.

## CHARACTERISTICS OF A GOOD LESSON AIM

Ask yourself the following questions to evaluate your lesson aim:

1. Is your lesson aim concise enough to be written down? Many teachers have a vague idea of a lesson aim, but it is not precise enough to be effective. You should be able to write your lesson aim clearly in a single sentence. Only then can it guide you in your lesson development.

2. Is your lesson aim specific enough to be attainable? Most lesson aims are too broad and too general. A good lesson aim focuses on specific areas in the students' lives where Bible truth can be put into practice. The response called for should be realistic enough to be achievable. The students should be able to begin the application process immediately.

3. Is your lesson aim flexible enough to be personalized? It is possible to make a lesson aim too specific. Because a teacher cannot know all the areas of need, the lesson aim should be flexible enough to permit the Holy Spirit to guide the learners to the unique response He chooses for them to make.

## Developing a Lesson Aim

Developing a lesson aim is the most difficult, yet the most important, part of lesson planning. Two factors must be considered. First, the aim should grow out of the meaning of the Bible passage or story. It is never legitimate to read into the Scriptures what they do not say. The aim should be based on sound principles of Bible interpretation. Second, the aim should be related to the students' needs. As stated earlier, the teacher must know the students' needs and where the lesson truth touches their lives.

Printed aims in the lesson materials can be a helpful resource as you develop your lesson aim. But no curriculum writer can structure an aim to meet everyone's needs. You will usually have to restate the aim to fit your students' needs.

## Developing the Lesson Plan

### Planning the Approach

After you know what you want to accomplish, plan a way to get your students involved in accomplishing the goal. People come to class with many things on their minds, so you must find a way to capture their attention and get them interested in the lesson. The first thing a good lesson approach does is to arouse interest and to lead naturally into the lesson. During the first few moments of the class session, you must get your students ready to discover Bible answers to their personal needs. Although the approach is the first part of the lesson plan, you may sometimes want to develop the rest of the lesson before deciding how you will get started.

### Planning the Bible Content

Now you are ready to move on to organizing the Bible content. Your purpose is to understand what the Bible has to say, what the passage or story is all about, and what solutions it has to offer to problems or situations. Your students need to know what the Bible teaches before they can apply it to their lives. One of your most important decisions in this part of the lesson is to determine what biblical materials to include and what to omit. The knowledge part of your lesson aim will serve as a guide in making these choices.

In addition to selecting your materials, you should also decide what methods you will be using. Try to include at least two or three different ways to present the lesson content so that student interest and involvement remain high.

### PLANNING THE APPLICATION

The application part of your lesson plan can be divided into two sections: personalizing the truth and planning for response. The first part of this two-step process is to help your students see the implications of the lesson truth for their lives. It is not enough for your students to know what the Bible says. You must lead them to see how its truths relate to them personally. Guide them in focusing on specific areas of application. The attitude part of your lesson aim will be accomplished here. Prayerfully plan this section of your lesson plan. Only the Holy Spirit knows the real needs of your students and only He can direct you to help make them aware of their needs.

The second part of the two-step process is to lead your students to respond to the lesson in some specific way. Again, it is not enough for them to know the Bible truth or even to see its implications for their lives. You must help them plan how to begin applying and acting on the lesson truth in everyday life. The conduct part of your lesson aim is carried out here. Carefully plan this part of the lesson. Do not leave it up to a spur-of-the-moment thought as the class period ends.

Lead your students to come to their own conclusions, guided by your gentle prodding and the convicting, convincing work of the Holy Spirit. Each student should decide on specific steps to begin responding to the lesson truth in the coming week. This part of the process too should not be hurried, so be sure to allow enough time. Build in reminders of the students' decisions. Follow up on the students in the next session to see if they did as planned.

## Planning Other Details

The following details of lesson planning should also be taken care of:

1. Plan the use of methods. Your lesson plan is accomplished through the use of many methods. Since learning is an active process for students, the best methods actively involve them. Each lesson plan should employ a variety of teaching techniques.

2. Prepare the teaching resources. Make sure you have available all the teaching aids you expect to use. By beginning your lesson planning early, you will have time to secure all the necessary supplies and to prepare all the resources. Organize your teaching materials in the order you plan to use them.

3. Assign student activities. Make student assignments far enough in advance so the students can adequately prepare. Follow up on the assignments during the week before they are due. Be sure to call for any assignments you make.

4. Plan the time schedule. As you develop your lesson plan, think through the schedule and estimate how much time each part will require. Write your schedule somewhere in your lesson plan in clock time rather than in lapsed time. For example, if your class session starts at 9:30 and your lesson-approach activity will take 10 minutes, write 9:40 in the left-hand margin at the point you begin the Bible content part of your outline. That way you can glance at your watch and know immediately where you are instead of having to compute the elapsed time and the time remaining.

5. Prepare the classroom. One of the strongest influences on your students is your classroom, so plan how to make it work best for you. Consider the following areas:

*Space needs*—The amount of room you have determines what methods and activities you can use. If the room is small, you may want to remove the table and use lapboards and wall space for writing and art activities.

*Sound levels*—The students should be able to hear clearly and without distractions. Use a small public-address system if you meet in a large room. Consider using carpeting or a throw rug to help absorb the sound. Work in cooperation with neighboring classes to eliminate interference.

*Lighting*—Check the lighting amount and distribution. You should also have some way to control the amount of light needed for different activities, such as doing handwork, worshiping, or viewing projected visuals. Avoid standing in front of a window or other bright light source because it creates a silhouette effect that obscures your facial expressions.

*Furnishings*—Tables and chairs should be the right size for each age-group. Be sure there are extra chairs for visitors. Repaint older furnishings to cover unsightly scars and scratches. Chalkboards, bulletin boards, pictures, and tack rails should be mounted at the students' eye level. Keep posted displays and announcements current.

*Decor*—Room colors greatly influence your students' attitudes and emotions. Oranges, reds, and yellows create a feeling of warmth, but tend to make a room seem smaller. Blues and greens create a more open, relaxed atmosphere and make a room appear larger. Wall posters can be used effectively to decorate your classroom. However, do not have bright bulletin boards or posters directly behind you; they will detract from your efforts.

*Air temperature and quality*—Maintaining good ventilation and an even temperature are important if you want to retain your students' attention and alertness. In the youth and adult departments, learning and involvement are enhanced when the room is slightly cool (68°). Rooms for small children should be kept at 70° or above. Promote air movement with fans, but be sure they have safety mesh small enough to prevent fingers from reaching the blades.

*Appearance*—Your classroom's general appearance also greatly influences your students. Have the room neatly arranged before the students arrive. The walls, floors, and window sills should be clean, and lighting fixtures and windows should be in working order. Try to keep papers and other materials from accumulating on tables and counters, on top of the piano, and elsewhere.

*Storage*—Ample storage space for learning resources, audiovisual equipment, and craft supplies is a must. Teachers should have lockable cabinets. Open shelving should be provided in the children's classrooms so the children can learn to put their materials away. Storage cabinets and closets should be frequently cleaned and rearranged.

## For Further Study

1. How does adequate preliminary planning make lesson planning more effective?
2. What happens when a teacher tries to cover too much material in a single lesson?
3. How do your lesson aims compare to the characteristics of a good lesson aim as discussed in this chapter?
4. What part does your lesson aim play in planning the Bible content of your lesson?
5. Why is it not enough for your students to know only the Bible content portion of your lesson?
6. What can you do to make your classroom a more effective learning environment?

# 6
# The Point of Effective Bible Teaching

Imagine preparing hot fudge sundaes for a group of your students while they watch. You put on all the fixings—chopped nuts, whipped cream, and cherries. Your students are riveted, mouths watering, but just when you are about to serve the treats, the bell rings. So you dump the sundaes in the garbage and send your students away!

You would never consider doing such a thing, but something similar happens every week in many Sunday school classes. A teacher spends 45 minutes preparing a beautiful dish of Bible truths, garnished with illustrations and visual aids. However, just when he should give his students something to take home with them, the bell rings and the lesson's impact is lost. The truth does little good because the students are not guided to apply it to their lives.

Although it is the students who must apply the lesson truth to their lives, you as the teacher have the responsibility of guiding them to discover and to begin responding to Bible truth so it can make a difference in their lives. Again, "The teacher has not taught until the student has learned."

The corollary to that statement is, "The student has not learned until he is putting into practice what he has learned." That means you cannot stop teaching after presenting the lesson content. You must also help your students to bridge the gap between the content and their personal needs. To do this "requires that we make a two-way journey. We begin by traveling from our own time and place to the ancient world of the

Bible. Then we take a return trip to our own experience of life."[1]

## Teaching for Change

Your students cannot respond to spiritual truth without undergoing some change. Change is a natural part of all growth. If there is no change, there is no growth. Learning itself is a change process. It involves changing facts, feelings, attitudes, and actions. Your goal should be to teach in such a way that it makes a difference in how your students live.

### RESISTANCE TO CHANGE

Although change is necessary and helpful, your students will not always agree. They may resist change for the following reasons:

1. *Loss of security*—The unknown and unfamiliar is frightening and unpredictable. The familiar is preferred, for people know what to expect. Seek to link new truths and actions with the tried and familiar. Change always proceeds from the known to the unknown.

2. *Loss of status or position*—Your students will resist change if they feel their vested interests are threatened in some way. Strive to assure them that what they are reaching for will be better than what they are leaving behind—that the difference will be worth the effort.

3. *Implied criticism of the status quo*—Advocating new ideas may suggest to some students a dissatisfaction with the way things are now. To overcome this, assure your students that you love and accept them as they are, while encouraging them to join you in growing together toward what God would have all of you to be.

4. *Unnecessary or unhelpful idea*—Some of your students may view their present situations as either satisfactory or utterly hopeless. They may resist an idea for change because a similar idea was once tried unsuccessfully. Two words can kill

any new idea, *never* and *always.* "We *never* did it that way before. We *always* did it this way." Help your students to see that change is needed and possible. Remind them that if God could change the lives of people in the Bible, He can do the same for them. An occasional personal evaluation form or questionnaire may help point out areas needing change.

## INITIATING CHANGE

You can do several things to make your students more receptive to the idea of change.

1. *Let your students share in the planning.* They will be more likely to accept change if they regard it as their idea and are involved in its implementation.

2. *Begin with small changes.* Work on one change at a time. Too often we address broad, general areas instead of zeroing in on a single area. Remind your students that sweeping changes start with a single step in the right direction.

3. *Develop a specific plan of action.* Help your students decide what, where, when, and how the changes can be made. Use a variety of approaches in developing your plans. Design some change activities as class projects, with everyone involved in the planning and completion of the project. At other times use small groups to share plans and ideas. Leave some plans to be developed on an individual basis.

4. *Be positive.* Students respond better to possibilities than to problems. Stress the benefits of the desired change without using pressure tactics.

5. *Watch your timing.* Be aware of any extenuating circumstances that may affect the outcome of suggested changes. Take note of the group atmosphere and the students' attitude.

6. *Keep the goal in focus.* Not only should the students be involved in making plans for change, but they should also keep their objective clearly in focus at all times. Evidence of progress toward the goal is the best motivation for more progress. Remember, nothing succeeds like success.

## TAPPING YOUR SPIRITUAL RESOURCES

As a Christian teacher, you have many spiritual resources at your disposal to initiate needed change. The Bible is filled with examples of leaders and teachers who brought about change. Let them be your inspiration. Remember to bathe your ideas in prayer, praying also for yourself and your students. Rely on the Holy Spirit's power to break down resistance to change, open closed minds, and create a readiness for change.

## Guiding Lesson Application

What happened during the closing 5 or 10 minutes of your class period last Sunday? Were you still trying to cover the rest of the lesson content? Did the class next door break out in boisterous activity, effectively ending any further teaching on your part? Maybe the class secretary began distributing the take-home papers. The closing moments of your class session are the most important in teaching to make a difference. That is when you should be guiding your students toward a personal application of the lesson to their life needs.

### TRADITIONAL APPROACHES TO LESSON APPLICATION

Three common approaches to secure lesson application are as follows:

1. *The Content Approach*—"I feel it is my job just to teach the lesson and to let the students decide for themselves how to apply the truths to their lives. I believe if the lesson is clearly and forcefully presented, the students will automatically put it into practice."

2. *The Illustration Approach*—"I always try to close the lesson with a story that illustrates how others have applied the Bible truth in their lives. Whenever I can, I give a personal example. I feel if my students see how others have responded to the Bible truth, they will want to do the same."

3. *The Generalization Approach*—"I always encourage my students to apply the lesson truths in their lives in the coming

week by closing with a few general suggestions for them to follow. Then I leave it up to them and the Holy Spirit to work things out."

But are these approaches really adequate? Do they result in change? Actually, each is flawed in some way. The first attempt often results in little actual change because the lessons do not automatically transfer from knowledge to experience. The second is somewhat better, but often works only if the situation in a student's life is very similar to the illustration used in class. It's just too easy for your students to forget all those wonderful examples when they encounter real-life issues. The third approach is ineffective because it lacks specificity. It does not help the students think through personal life situations and offers no assistance in making plans to implement the lesson truths in the coming week.

GUIDED SELF-APPLICATION

In his book *Creative Bible Teaching,* Lawrence Richards suggests an approach to lesson application that is much more effective in helping bring about real change in the students' lives. He calls it "Guided Self-Application."[2] It involves the following five-step process:

1. Lead the students in reviewing and restating the biblical principle on which the lesson is developed. This step is important because it helps you know whether or not your students understand what the Bible says. It also helps you focus on a single lesson truth rather than trying to cover all the truths that could be taught in the lesson.

2. Guide the students in seeing several areas of their lives where the biblical principle applies. This step helps the students bridge the gap between their world and the world of the Bible. The first part of the lesson application (personalizing the lesson), discussed in the previous chapter, is developed in this step. Remember, your goal is to help your students see the lesson's relevance to their own situations.

3. Lead the students in focusing on one area for personal exploration. If the students try to apply the biblical principle to every need in their lives, little change will occur. Instead, help them to focus on a single area needing change. This makes the process of change less foreboding and more attainable.

4. Guide the students in planning how to act on the lesson truth in one area of their lives. This can be done, as suggested earlier, with the class as a whole, in small groups, or individually. The second part of the application process (planning for response) is accomplished in this step.

5. Encourage and help the students in carrying out their application plans during the coming week. Help the students understand that they are expected to put their good intentions into practice. Make some efforts to follow up on their plans right there in class. However, since the action response will usually take place sometime during the coming week, let the students know that they will be asked to report next week on their efforts at lesson application. As someone has observed, you get what you *inspect,* not what you *expect.*

The following lesson plan shows how this approach to guiding lesson application could work with a class of middlers (ages 8 and 9) studying the lesson of Jesus and Zaccheus. Our three-part aim for the session is (1) to know that Jesus loved Zaccheus, (2) to feel that Jesus loves and accepts us as much, and (3) to show love and kindness to people who are different from us. (The parts of the lesson plan are numbered to correspond with the five-step applicational approach.)

1. Have some students draw pictures of different scenes from the story on large sheets of paper taped to the walls. Have another group practice acting out the Bible story. Have a third group look through old magazines for pictures of people who are different from them.

2. Lead the students in conversation, asking the following questions: What are some ways we are all different from each other? Are there times when it's not fun to be different? How

do you feel when you think you are different from everyone else? How do you think other people feel when they realize they are different from others?

3. Ask each student to think of someone he will see next week who is different from him. Have him draw a picture of that person.

4. Brainstorm on ways the students could be kind to those people. Help them come up with specific things they could do, such as playing with them, sharing things with them, inviting them to their homes, or perhaps calling them on the telephone.

5. Distribute paper and envelopes and ask the students to write a short letter to themselves telling what they will do this week to show kindness to those individuals. Collect the envelopes and mail them to the students on Monday. Ask them next Sunday what happened when they showed kindness.

The following lesson plan shows how the applicational approach would work with a class of adults studying the Beatitudes in Matthew 5. Our three-part aim for the session is (1) to know that Jesus calls us to be salt and light in our world, (2) to desire to be a positive influence in our world, and (3) to determine to change to be good examples. (Again the parts of the lesson plan are numbered to correspond with the five-step applicational approach.)

1. Divide the class into two groups. Assign Group 1 to compile a list of ways Christians are like salt in the world. Assign Group 2 to compile a list of ways Christians are like light in the world.

2. Lead the class in discussing ways the Beatitudes call for behavior that is quite different from the world's. List these on the chalkboard or an overhead transparency.

3. Distribute 3- by 5-inch cards and ask each student to write one behavior that is the most difficult to carry out. Explain that the students will be asked to reveal what they wrote to one other person.

4. Lead the students in brainstorming for a list of things that would help them live the Beatitudes in daily life. Encourage

them to be specific. List their ideas on the chalkboard or an overhead transparency.

5. Ask each person to write two or three ideas suggested by the class that would help him change the one difficult behavior he wrote earlier. Ask the students to share what they wrote with one other person and pray with each other before leaving the classroom.

## ADVANTAGES OF THIS APPROACH

Using the guided self-application approach in teaching is far more likely to bring about change than using the traditional methods of lesson application. For example, the story of Zaccheus will be more personal if the students think of it in terms of people who are different from themselves. Planning ways to be kind to such people is more meaningful than merely hearing a story about someone else's actions and being told to do the same. It will result in a more in-depth study of the Beatitudes and a more personalized lesson. Sharing and praying together also add a measure of accountability.

The advantages of this approach to lesson application are obvious. Because the students are made personally responsible for applying the lesson truth, they not only will remember the experience far longer than a teacher-oriented lesson, but also will be more likely to act on the truth. Furthermore, the students learn for themselves how to apply Bible truth to life—a skill they can later use on their own.

## CHANGES REQUIRED BY THIS APPROACH

The applicational approach not only requires your students to change, but also requires you to alter your teaching in several ways.

1. *Your use of time*—The applicational process takes more time than just a few minutes at the end of the lesson. The students need time to reach their own conclusions on the lesson's implications for their lives and the decisions they must

make. Teens and adults may require up to half the class time for lesson application. Younger children will obviously need less time since they are unable to explore implications. With preschool students, the lesson truth should be applied on the spot. For example, if the Bible truth emphasizes that God hears our prayers, the teacher and children should pray frequently during the hour to reinforce that truth. If the lesson truth is God wants us to help, the children should be given several opportunities to help during the class.

The following chart indicates the amount of time needed for lesson application for each of the four major age-groups:

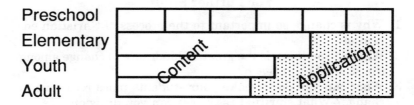

2. *Your role as a teacher*—Instead of being a dispenser of information, be a guide. You cannot order your students to apply the lesson to their lives; you can only guide them. You cannot force them to follow through on their plans; you can only encourage them. Your students still need your help and ideas, but they must be led to their own conclusions and decisions.

3. *Your use of methodology*—You cannot lecture your way through the applicational approach. It simply won't work. The methods you use must involve your students. Look back at some of the methods used in the sample lesson plans. They include guided conversation, letter writing, small-group assignments, brainstorming, prayer-and-share groups, etc. Other methods that work well are questionnaires and opinionnaires, personal evaluations, written prayer reminders, open-ended stories, roleplays, art activities, and group discussions.

## In Summary

It is absolutely essential that you think of your teaching in terms of bringing about change in the students' attitudes and actions. Discovering new biblical truth without doing anything about it is disastrous. That's why you must guide your students to apply biblical truth and think of ways to help them follow through with their plans during the week. If you teach in this manner, you will see your students grow toward real maturity in Christ, and discover the delight of being engaged in teaching for change. That, after all, is the real point of effective Bible teaching—to make a difference in your students' lives.

## For Further Study

1. Why is change so important to the process of Christian education?
2. What do you think is the greatest hindrance to change among the students you teach?
3. What can you do to make your students more receptive to change? What spiritual resources can you draw on?
4. Why are some of the traditional approaches to lesson application ineffectual? What results have you observed when you have tried some of those approaches?
5. How is the guided self-application approach different from the approaches most teachers use?
6. What do you think is the greatest advantage of this approach?
7. What changes would you have to make in your teaching to use this applicational approach?

### NOTES

[1]Jim Wilhoit and Leland Ryken, *Effective Bible Teaching* (Grand Rapids, Mich.: Baker Book House, 1988), 96.

[2]Lawrence O. Richards, *Creative Bible Teaching* (Chicago: Moody Press, 1970), 119.

# 7

# The Practical Aspects of Effective Bible Teaching

Let's pay another visit to our two teachers, Fred and Mark, whom you met in chapter 5.

THE SCENE: A hallway outside their classrooms
THE TIME: The end of the Sunday school hour

FRED: I'm glad that's over for another week! My students get so restless. I just can't seem to hold their attention.

MARK: Really? My students and I got so involved in the lesson, I hated to hear the bell ring.

FRED: I try to get my students to participate, but they just sit there. What do you do to get them so involved?

MARK: Well, I've found that my students learn best when they are purposefully involved in the session, so I try to use methods that require their participation.

FRED: My students are active all right, but not with anything that has to do with the lesson. This morning I had to chase two of them out from behind the piano.

MARK: That's where the right kind of motivation helps. I try to tap my students' interests and needs.

FRED: The only thing my students seem to be interested in is disrupting the lesson.

MARK: My students were like that once too, until I learned the secret of using teaching methods that closely relate to the way they learn.

Which teacher in this dialogue do you identify with? Your answer will reveal a lot about the methods you use. Your basic stock in trade as a teacher is your methodology—that's where the practical aspects of effective teaching come into play.

## Using Methods in Teaching

Every Bible teacher uses methods in his teaching. Some teachers use a wide variety of methods quite effectively. Others use only a few methods with varying degrees of effectiveness. Methods are an indispensable part of any meaningful teaching-learning experience. Without them a teacher cannot teach. *How* students learn greatly influences *what* they learn. Through your use of methods, you could be teaching things you are not even aware of. For example, if the discovery of Bible truths is not made interesting and enjoyable, your students will regard the Bible as boring and irrelevant.

The methods you use also affect the impact of your teaching. An old Chinese proverb says:

> I hear and I forget.
> I see and I remember.
> I do and I understand.

Your students will remember and understand the things they do in class much longer than the things they only hear.

### DEFINING METHODS

Methods are the means used to accomplish a task or to meet an objective. Teaching methods are the means to fulfilling your educational goals. Bible teaching methods are the means by which you and your students interact with the truths of God's Word.

In defining methods, think of them more as *learning* methods than as *teaching* methods. Although this may seem like a minor difference in terminology, it really is more important than that. If you view methods as primarily *teaching* methods, your choice of methods will be based on your personal preference. However, if you see methods as *learning* methods, you will base your choice on what will best help your students to learn.

Methods are merely a means to an end, not an end in themselves. Some teachers become so engrossed with the methodology of their task, they lose sight of their ultimate purpose, to see their students grow toward maturity in Christ.

## THE BEST METHOD

Teachers sometimes ask, "What is the best method to use with my students?" There are no simple answers, but two basic principles apply.

1. Use the methods that most closely relate to the way your students learn. For example, if they learn best through activity, use methods that actively involve them in the learning process, such as assignments and projects, group discussions, writing activities, taking a trip. If your students learn best through their senses, use methods that appeal to a wide variety of sensorial experiences, such as seeing projected visuals, touching an object, tasting a piece of fruit. If your students learn best by being motivated, the most effective methods will appeal to their needs and interests; for example, case studies, roleplays, character comparisons, questionnaires.

2. Use a variety of methods. Even the best, most creative methods lose their effectiveness if used too often. A combination of methods is best. A simple rule of thumb is to try to use at least three different methods in each session.

## SELECTING METHODS

In selecting methods, consider the following factors:

1. *Objectives*—Ask yourself, "Will this method help me accomplish my aims for this session?" If the answer is no, discard the method, no matter how appealing it may be. Or use the method and rewrite your objectives.

2. *Age and abilities*—Obviously, not all methods are appropriate for every age-group. Ask yourself, "Can my students do

this activity? Will they find it meaningful?" Teachers turn off students when they use methods that are either too juvenile for their age or too demanding.

3. *Time schedule*—Some methods take more time than others. Ask yourself, "Do I have enough time to use this method effectively? Will the learning outcome be worth the investment of additional time?" Do not discard good methods simply because they take time. Your students will remember the things they do far longer than the things they hear.

4. *Facilities and equipment*—Some methods require additional space or special equipment. Ask yourself, "Will this approach work in my classroom or department? Do I have the special equipment or supplies I will need?" If it is a good method, look for creative ways to incorporate it into your teaching.

Ask yourself the same questions about the methods suggested in the curriculum materials. Only you can determine if the suggested activities will work in your situation. Usually you will have to modify the ideas somewhat to fit your class' needs. Keep a list of methods, such as those given in this chapter. It will serve as a helpful resource in choosing alternative activities.

## CATEGORIZING METHODS

Methods can be categorized in several ways. Following is a list of methods *grouped by objectives.*

1. Methods designed to gain information:
   | | |
   |---|---|
   | Storytelling | Panel |
   | Question and answer | Symposium |
   | Lecture | Research report |
2. Methods designed to gain opinions about an issue:
   | | |
   |---|---|
   | Circle response | Questionnaire |
   | Group discussion | Group writing project |
   | Class survey | Anonymous poll |
3. Methods designed to secure solutions to a problem:

Brainstorming              Roleplay
Case study                 Simulation games
Buzz groups              Field trip

4. Methods designed to encounter biblical truths:

Choral Bible reading      Filmstrip
Inductive Bible study      Scripture paraphrase
Narrative Scripture reading Concordance search

5. Methods designed to encourage creative expression:

Clay modeling           Designing bumper stickers
Collage or montage        Writing a newspaper story
Individual art or writing   Songwriting
Acting out a story

6. Methods designed to accomplish a task:

Written assignments     Group project
Planning teams           How-to demonstration

Another way to categorize methods is to group them according to the *part of the lesson* in which they will be used.

1. Methods used in getting started:

Agree/disagree           Skit
Graffiti poster           Interview
Neighbor nudging       Picture search

2. Methods used in communicating Bible content:

Parallel Scripture reading  Bible dramatization
Storytelling              Listening teams
Character comparisons   Directed group Bible study
Symposium                Research report

3. Methods used in securing lesson application:

Guided conversation     Personal evaluations
Writing activities        Written prayer reminders
Group projects            Individual art activities
Case studies              Brainstorming

A third way to categorize methods is to group them according to the *types of methods* they are.

1. Lecture methods:

Research and report
Guest speaker
Dialogue interview
Debate
Cassette recording

Symposium
Current events
Bible story video
Monologue
Listening teams

2. Discussion methods:

Expanding panel
Dyads
Brainstorming
Circle response
Case studies

Open-ended stories
Buzz groups
Agree/disagree
Group discussion
Direct group Bible study

3. Drama methods:

Skits
Narrative readings
Pantomimes
Pageants
Tableaus
Demonstrations

Period interviews
Roleplays
Videotaped enactment
Newscasts
Puppets
TV script

4. Art methods:

Banners and posters
Bumper stickers
Campaign buttons
Cartoon strips
Collages and montages
Time line
Medieval coat of arms

Graffiti poster
Graphs and charts
Murals
Maps
Rebus
Frieze
Road of life

5. Writing activities:

Acrostic
Written prayers
Log or journal
Reaction sheet
Tests and quizzes
Newspaper story

Scripture paraphrase
Letter writing
Word puzzle
Rankings
Word association
Poetry

6. Music methods:

Hymn paraphrase
Lyric writing
Song title list

Musical commercial
Song comparison
Songwriting

An unending list of creative methods can be used to enhance teaching and learning. The lists on pages 80–82 are just a sample. Some methods may be new to you; others will be familiar. We will discuss some methods in more detail in the next two chapters on teaching different age-groups.

Methods are the tools of your trade as a teacher. You cannot function without them. Make a personal study of the techniques that relate to your age-group. Stay alert to new ideas you pick up in reading good books and other resources on the subject. Also, talk to other teachers and find out what works and what doesn't work for them. Listen to your students. They may provide important clues on how they are being taught in school, through on-the-job training, or in continuing education programs.

## Using Audiovisual Methods

Your students live in a multimedia world. From the time they awake until they go to bed, they are bombarded by sights and sounds. Often, this is the situation in all but one setting—the Bible classroom—where they are treated as if only one sensory channel exists, hearing. Yet, as the figures in chapter 4 revealed, learning is greatly enhanced when a combination of senses is involved.

Audiovisual methods serve several important purposes in effective teaching.

1. Audiovisuals arouse and retain the students' interest. Every time you hold up a picture or turn on the overhead projector you refocus your students' attention.

2. Audiovisuals clarify words and ideas. As a teacher you encounter certain barriers in Bible teaching, one of which is the *time and space barrier.* Because Bible events happened a long time ago and in a place far removed from our world, you must help your students understand the setting and culture of Bible events. Audiovisuals can help you to do that.

Another barrier is *language and jargon.* Teachers are sometimes guilty of using terms that are familiar to them, but not to their students. Again, audiovisual methods can help overcome this barrier.

3. Audiovisuals provide a common experience and stimulate thought and discussion. Viewing the same video or constructing a graffiti poster gives the class something to talk about. Input flows freely from this enjoyable way of learning together.

4. Audiovisuals provide an effective means for review and repetition. Flipping through last week's picture cards or recounting a mural scene are great ways to reinforce learning. When such visuals are the product of the students' own creative efforts, so much the better.

## NONPROJECTED VISUALS

### The Chalkboard

A widely available and versatile visual aid, the chalkboard is a valuable resource. It appeals to all ages, is inexpensive, does not require extensive preparation, and can be used by both teachers and students. Two types of chalkboards are available, wall-mounted and portable. Your church should be equipped with both types. Chalkboards should be the proper size for the group. Boards in larger classrooms and auditoriums should measure 4 by 6 feet, and boards in smaller rooms at least 2 by 4 feet. All chalkboards should be mounted at the students' eye level.

Keep in mind the following techniques when using the chalkboard:

1. Think through what you will print or draw. Have a basic layout in mind.
2. Write clearly and large enough for all the students to see. Using correct spelling is also important. Use abbreviations only if they are plainly understood.
3. Put large amounts of material on the board before class begins. Cover the portions you do not want to be seen with strips of paper backed with loops of masking tape.

4. Keep the chalk from squeaking by holding it at a sharp angle. Keep the board and erasers clean.
5. To draw a straight line, mark two points and, keeping your eye focused on the second point, draw the line. To draw a circle, step back an arm's length and draw it in one complete motion starting at the top.
6. Use colored chalk to add variety and emphasis.

The chalkboard is an effective tool for you and an excellent way to involve your students. For example, let the students draw scenes from the Bible story, or ask a student who prints clearly to record the class' comments as you lead the discussion. Let the students practice drawing simple Bible maps and finding the locations under discussion.

### Posters and Banners

Posters make effective teaching tools because their bold design catches and holds the students' attention long enough to implant or reinforce a significant idea. Posters can be inexpensively prepared for any occasion, reflect a personal touch, provide valuable and creative group experiences, and express biblical truth in a contemporary format.

Some basic characteristics of good posters are simplicity, attractiveness, design, color, contrast, originality, and size. A poster should be simple, yet striking enough to attract attention and to convey the message quickly.

Supplies needed for making posters include poster board or tablecloth paper, colored construction paper, broad-tipped marking pens, crayons or poster paint, rulers, lettering guides, scissors, glue, and pictures. Three-dimensional items such as plastic flowers, pipe cleaners, small toys, and dolls can also be used.

Consider the following ideas for different kinds of posters:[1]

1. *A calendar poster*—Mount a page from a large calendar on a colored background. In the square for the date you are

emphasizing, letter the name of the event, time, place, etc. Draw a series of hands or arrows pointing to the square.

2. *A see-through poster*—Print, paint, or glue a message on a clear sheet of acetate or a roll of clear plastic wrap, and suspend it in a window or doorway. Or make a mounting frame by cutting the center out of a large piece of cardboard or poster board and taping the poster to the backside of the frame.

3. *A supermarket poster*—Ask a supermarket manager to save some of his discarded posters. Use them as background for your own posters. Cut out or cover up unrelated words and insert your own. Use the illustrations on the posters (e.g., bread, fruit, desserts, meats) as part of your poster message.

4. *A box poster*—Randomly stack a number of cardboard boxes of different sizes. Cover each exposed surface with bright colored paper and mount photographs, pictures, or cutout or printed letters on each one. Occasionally rearrange the boxes in the shape of a square, pyramid, or column.

Banners also have many uses in Bible teaching. The two types of banners are cloth, made for a permanent display, and paper, used as a temporary teaching tool.

To make a permanent banner you will need a large piece of heavy cloth, such as burlap, muslin, or vinyl, and small pieces of other types of cloth in various colors and textures. First, make a sketch of how the banner is to look. Second, make large patterns of the various letters and figures and arrange them on the background material. Third, cut out the individual items and sew or glue them on the banner. Finally, make a 2-inch hem at the top for a rod or cord. Loops may also be sewn to the top of the banner to accommodate a rod.

Many different types of paper banners can be used in the classroom.

1. A *mural* is a large picture or combination of pictures that tells a story or portrays something with many interrelated parts. It may be created as one large piece, or the students may work on individual sections and assemble them later. Use mu-

rals to re-create Bible scenes such as the 6 days of creation, to summarize a Bible story such as Christmas or Easter, to create a worship background, to visualize a variety of prayer needs, to tell about your community, or to highlight special events.

2. A *frieze* is a series or sequence of pictures or cartoon figures that tells a continuous story. It is usually drawn on a long sheet of paper. Use a frieze to review a Bible story, to show events in a missionary's life, to show how we got our Bible, or to visualize events from church history.

3. A *graffiti poster* is a selection of writings, slogans, drawings, symbols, or cartoons that focuses on a particular theme. It works best with older children, youth, or young adults. To make a graffiti poster, attach a long strip of paper to a wall near the entrance to your classroom. Write the poster's theme (e.g., "Reasons To Be Thankful") at the top and ask arriving students to write or draw something on the poster that expresses their thoughts or impressions on the theme. Use graffiti posters to introduce a lesson, to determine the students' attitudes, or to relate a Bible subject to everyday life.

4. A *montage* is a collection of individual pictures, articles, headlines, or ads arranged to form a composite picture or design. Use a montage to help the students relate Bible truths to daily life. Involve the students in selecting and arranging a variety of graphic images to capture a particular theme or idea.

5. A *collage* is similar to a montage, but it uses three-dimensional items, such as leaves, sticks, pebbles, scraps of cloth, and small toys. Use a collage or montage to show things God has made, to re-create a biblical scene, to show the Bible's relevance to current events, to apply biblical principles to real-life situations, to introduce a lesson series, or to portray the different sides of an issue.

## PROJECTED VISUALS

### Overhead Projector

The overhead projector is the most versatile projection device available today. Its advantages are obvious. The teacher can face the students, thus maintaining eye contact. The overhead projector can be used in a fully or partially lighted room. Transparencies can be made beforehand and preserved for future use. Overlays (more than one layer of transparencies) and sliding masks (pieces of paper moved down the transparency to reveal one line at a time) can be used to show the development of ideas, to control the group's attention, and to keep the class from reading ahead of you. The large transparency format (10 by 10 inches) is easy to use. Even young children can draw or write on it. And the horizontal stage can be used to project small objects in silhouette.

The simplest way to prepare an overhead transparency is to write directly on a sheet or roll of acetate with a felt-tipped pen. A grid sheet or a sheet of lined notebook paper may be placed beneath the transparency to keep the lines and letters even.

Most office copy machines can be used to make overhead transparencies. Special transparency acetate is available from a manufacturer or an office supply store. Transparency copies can be run through the machine much as paper copies are.

The color-lift process is an interesting way to make transparencies. Through this process, pictures and other graphics printed on clay-coated paper can be directly transferred to adhesive-backed acetate. To see if the image you want to copy is printed on clay-coated paper, wet your fingertip and gently rub it on a blank space on the paper. If a white, milky residue appears on your finger, the paper is clay-coated.

Cut a piece of adhesive-backed acetate slightly larger than the picture. Laminating plastic can be used for this. Remove the backing from the acetate and place it over the picture. Press the acetate smoothly over the picture and rub out any air bubbles, using a smooth, hard instrument such as the back of a spoon. Rub firmly in all directions to ensure a tight fit between the acetate and the paper.

Next, place the picture-and-acetate sandwich into a pan of warm water containing a mild detergent. Leave it there until the acetate begins to separate from the paper fiber. Usually the picture can be peeled away quite easily. Sometimes gentle rubbing may be necessary. Rinse off any remaining clay residue or bits of paper fiber. You can now rub the acetate gently without fear of smudging the ink. Air-dry the acetate and mount it in a transparency frame. If you want to preserve your color-lift acetate, spray the adhesive side with a clear fixative spray to seal the surface.

In addition to the usual uses of the overhead projector, it also has some creative uses. Make a poster or enlarge a diagram by making a transparency of the original and projecting it onto a poster board or a sheet of construction paper. Trace the outline with a transparency pen. Cartoons or comic strips can be enlarged the same way.

Use the overhead projector to project a picture or sketch onto a classroom wall to provide a guide in making murals or other decorations. Provide blank transparencies and marking pens for discussion groups to use in compiling reports from their discussions. Create a special-effects background by putting a few drops of different colors of food coloring between two damp transparencies. Then stick the transparencies together.

Give the students blank transparencies and a supply of small magnetic or adhesive-backed letters to use in forming words. Or let them use toothpicks, Q-tips, or matchsticks to create figures in silhouette.

Play a game of Bible tic-tac-toe by drawing the lines on a transparency and using different shaped objects to mark the positions of the two teams or individuals.

## Videos

The videocassette recorder (VCR) has become a readily available audiovisual teaching aid. Videos have many benefits and uses in the classroom.

1. Videos combine sight and sound in a single medium.
2. Videos give the most lifelike presentation.
3. Videos provide immediate repetition and review.

4. Videos can be stopped at any time to allow class participation.
5. Videos are widely available.
6. Videos can be recorded easily and inexpensively.
7. Videos are easy to operate.

Videocassettes can be shown by using several different kinds of equipment. In a smaller classroom or assembly area use a VCR and a portable television set or monitor. In a larger auditorium, connect several monitors to the same VCR, or use a large-screen video projector.

Keep in mind the following principles when planning to use videos:

1. *Preparation*—Select video materials on the basis of their ability to help you accomplish specific learning goals. In other words, don't show a video just to fill time. Be sure to preview the material. That will help you to make a proper introduction. Develop a few listening questions to give the students before the presentation. Note stopping points to permit discussion or other class participation. Set up and check all necessary equipment beforehand. Dimming the lights may help eliminate screen glare. Make sure the video is properly cued.

2. *Presentation*—Give a brief introduction to the video and explain your purpose in showing it. Make sure everyone can see and hear clearly. You may want to divide the class into several groups and give each team a listening assignment. When you come to the end of the presentation, turn down the sound before turning off the recorder.

3. *Follow-up*—Call for reports from the listening teams. Lead the students in discussing what they witnessed, and help them to think through how its principles can be applied to their lives. Clear up any misconceptions and direct the students to any other materials on the subject. Be sure to return all the equipment and videos to their proper storage place.

Consider using videos or video cameras in the following ways:

1. To supplement the Sunday school or children's church Bible story
2. To augment small-group or home Bible studies
3. To add variety to class presentations
4. To record man-on-the-street interviews
5. To record students' responses to a set of discussion questions in a learning center
6. To produce your own Bible story—use teams of students to write the script, play the roles, shoot the video, and set up the equipment for viewing
7. To provide training videos for prospective teachers to view at home
8. To record training sessions for absent staff members
9. To present premarital counseling
10. To communicate with missionaries during missions conventions or to show their work on the field
11. To introduce visitors to your church's ministries and programs
12. To view community needs or local institutions—assign a group of students to record scenes to bring back and show the class
13. To show music videos of popular gospel singers at a youth or young adult party
14. To videotape the class session or church service to take to shut-ins
15. To videotape the class session to evaluate your effectiveness as a teacher
16. To set up a video booth at a fair, shopping center, or other community location
17. To set up a video recorder and monitor in the church foyer to promote a special program or activity
18. To sponsor a summer children's festival or youth video festival at church or at a community location
19. To air videos of church services and special teaching seminars on the public access channels of local cable TV companies
20. To use the visual portion of videos showing national shrines

and scenic views as a backdrop for a special patriotic musical presentation.

## For Further Study

1. Why is it important to think of methods as learning methods rather than as teaching methods?
2. What have you found to be the best methods in teaching your group? Why are they effective?
3. What barriers do you encounter in Christian teaching? How can audiovisuals help overcome them?
4. What are some ways you can involve your students in using the chalkboard?
5. What are some creative ways to use posters and banners?
6. What are some ways to make overhead transparencies?
7. Why are videocassettes such effective teaching tools?

### NOTES

[1]Adapted from *Making Nonprojected Visuals and Displays,* by Mancil Ezell (Nashville, Tenn.: Broadman Press, 1975), 41–47.

# 8

# Providing Bible Teaching
# for Younger Learners
# (Preschool and Elementary)

We often speak of the happy, carefree days of childhood. We reflect on it as one of the most enjoyable periods of our lives. But children today are growing up in a world vastly different from the one we knew. For many of them, childhood is anything but happy and carefree. Some, unfortunately, experience a lifetime of heartache before even reaching their teen years. They know firsthand about the stress and distress of life long before they should.

## Meeting the Needs of Today's Children

### DIVORCE

One of every two marriages still ends in divorce. Children are the innocent, tragic victims. "The trends indicate that of all the children born in 1990, six out of ten will live in a single-parent household for some period of time before they reach the age of 18."[1]

Some children cope relatively well with the trauma of divorce, but many others exhibit academic, emotional, social, and behavioral problems. Many children from broken homes are angry and frustrated because they view their parents' divorce as unnecessary. They feel their parents separated only to satisfy purely personal, selfish desires, with little regard for their welfare. Such children come into your classroom with intense feelings of rejection, guilt, insecurity, hostility, loneliness, low self-esteem, and withdrawal.

Another side effect of divorce is economic hardship. Single

parenthood and poverty often go hand in hand, especially in households headed by single mothers. According to some reports, almost 35 percent of such families live below the poverty level.

## TWO-INCOME FAMILIES

More than half of all mothers with preschool and elementary-age children work outside the home. More than 10 million children age 6 and younger spend all or part of their day in child-care facilities. Another 10 million children under age 13 are left unsupervised at home for a significant part of each day. These latchkey children return to an empty house or apartment every day.

## CHILD ABUSE

A tragedy of our times is the brutal abuse of children at the hands of, or in the presence of, their own parents. Reported cases of child maltreatment continue soaring, with some states marking increases from 28 to 46 percent in a single year.

## CHILDHOOD STRESS SYNDROME

Pediatricians report treating more stress-related ailments among children. One alarming trend is the increase of child suicide, up 150 percent in recent years among children ages 5 to 14. In an attempt to deal with stress, children are turning to drug use, alcoholism, and sexual promiscuity, which have risen dramatically among children. Homes for unwed mothers report children as young as 11 years old among their residents.

Children are also facing another more subtle, but equally devastating form of stress, the pressure to grow up quickly. They are being pressured to look and act like miniature adults and are encouraged to engage in adult-style competitive sports at increasingly younger ages. Even 3- and 4-year-old children are being organized into teams and cheered on by parents who desperately want them to win.

Children also experience considerable academic pressure. Being average is not acceptable anymore. Often, there is no room for the late bloomer. Sadly, much of this pressure to succeed comes from the parents themselves, who seek vicarious ego satisfaction through their children's accomplishments. Other parents simply want their children to grow up so they can get on with their own interests and pursuits.

Our children need help! We must understand what they are facing and come to their aid. The following things will help your teaching make a vital difference in children's lives:

1. *Know and love your students as individuals.* You have no idea what needs and problems they encounter when they leave your classroom. Some may deal daily with the very pressures and abuses already described. You may be the only adult in their lives who really loves and cares for them and takes time for them.

2. *Turn down the heat.* Children live with enough pressures at home and school. They shouldn't have to face more of the same at church. Of course, you want them to learn and accomplish certain things, but try to find ways to encourage them to learn without exerting undue pressure. Let them learn at their own rate and in their own ways. Evaluate the games and contests you offer, and try to reduce the level of competition and the pressure to win.

3. *Seek to train and influence the parents to be more aware of and sensitive to their children.* Because you cannot undo all the effects of home and society in 1 or 2 hours of Sunday school and church, you must look for ways to reach and teach the parents. Schedule a seminar so you can share the insights and information you have gained about children's needs. Set up individual parent-teacher conferences to discuss your observations, concerns, and recommendations.

The Bible teaches that children are a gift from God. They are too precious to be pressured and prodded, used and abused. The biblical warning to those who do so is quite specific: they would be better off if a millstone were tied around their neck and they were thrown into a deep sea. Childhood should be a happy, carefree time. You can make it so for the children God has placed in your care. Your teaching can make a great difference as you shape and mold the children's lives.

## Teaching Children the Way They Learn

Childhood presents you with one of life's greatest teaching-learning opportunities. Your success will be determined to a great extent by your ability to tap into the children's natural learning characteristics. Keep in mind the following:

1. *Children are naturally curious.* They are anxious to learn everything they can about their world, and their interests are practically unlimited. Of course, the scope of their curiosity and interests will be as varied as the number of children in your class. Therefore, you should present the students with different ways to learn. Interest centers are a natural for children because they provide a variety of learning approaches and activities. Learning centers also encourage the students to develop their own unique skills and abilities.

2. *Children are naturally creative.* They are constantly coming up with new words for a song or a different way to play a familiar game. Often their creativity is expressed in their fascinating world of make-believe. Tap into this creative energy by encouraging them to think for themselves and to plan some of their own learning activities.

3. *Children are naturally active.* They have a God-given need to be on the move. Trying to keep them corralled around a table for more than a few minutes at a time is nearly impossible, so use their restlessness to your advantage. Let them march around Jericho, as Joshua and the Children of Israel did. Have them act out the story of the Good Samaritan. Tape a strip of paper to the wall and have the children re-create scenes from the story of Paul's trip to Damascus.

4. *Children are naturally friendly.* This is one of the delights of working with them. They actually like you! So get to know

them, and let them get to know you. Children are fascinating creatures. Look for opportunities to spend time with them outside the classroom. As they become your friends, you will have an open door to tell them about your other friend, Jesus.

5. *Children are naturally spiritual.* They are as interested in the world of the Spirit as they are in any other dimension of their lives. Children are very sensitive to God's presence and can be taught to respond in ways that please Him. Their honesty and sense of fairness helps them understand their need of a Savior. Their tenderheartedness causes them to be concerned about the needs of others. Thus, children can be taught and trained in a way that will make a difference for all time and eternity.

## More Methods for Children

### USING STORIES

One of the most effective ways to teach children is through stories. Stories are an enjoyable way of conveying biblical truth and helping the students apply it to their lives. Stories help children see the results of good and bad choices made by the characters. Stories help change attitudes, stimulate emotions, develop the imagination, cultivate good listening habits, and enlarge the children's world of experience. Stories can be used to (1) introduce a lesson, (2) illustrate a point, (3) apply the lesson to life, (4) lead into worship, (5) introduce a song, or (6) aid in Scripture memorization.

When selecting stories for preschoolers, remember they like stories about things that are familiar to them, such as pets, babies, and family life. Bible stories for this age-group should be carefully chosen. They should be no longer than 2 to 5 minutes (the group's attention span) and should be limited to one main thought or idea.

Younger elementary children like fantasy stories, while the older ones prefer more realistic, true-to-life stories. Nearly all Bible stories are appropriate for these ages. Again, the stories should not be longer than the group's attention span (6 to 11 minutes for elementary children).

Keep in mind the following principles when telling stories:

1. Assume a natural position in front of the class. With younger children it may be better to sit down. Maintain eye contact and be sure to hold all visual materials at the students' eye level.
2. Use a few natural gestures, but try to avoid distracting mannerisms. Let your facial expressions aid you in conveying feelings and attitudes.
3. Be enthusiastic. Make the story come alive.
4. Vary the pace and volume of your delivery. Use an occasional dramatic pause to heighten suspense and to refocus the children's attention.
5. Change the tone of your voice to represent the different characters in the story. That will make it unnecessary to say repeatedly, "And Paul said . . .," "And the soldier said . . . ."
6. Use words the children can easily understand, but don't talk down to them. Simple action words are best.
7. Enunciate your words clearly and articulately. Project your voice so everyone can hear.
8. Know the story well enough so you can tell it and not read it.

Stories are not only an effective way for teachers to teach, but also a great way to involve the students in the teaching-learning process. Children are natural storytellers, so let them tell a story occasionally. With your help, they can become proficient storytellers. Begin by helping them select the right story to tell. It should be one they can tell in their own words. Explain to the children the different parts of the story (introduction, body, and climax) and help them understand the plot. They may find it helpful to make a pictorial outline and to practice telling the story in front of a mirror. Encourage the students to try using some of the storytelling principles previously discussed. Do everything you can to ensure that the children's first attempt is successful, but let the students know it's only natural to stumble over a word here and there.[2]

There are several other ways to involve your children in storytelling. Let them act out the story. Little or no costuming is necessary. However, since children like to dress up, by cutting down a few old bathrobes and using some towels, you can outfit most Bible characters. Encourage the students to draw scenes from the story or to model them with clay or cardboard cutouts. Let the children tell the story and put the figures on the flannelboard, or have them make paper-bag puppets of the characters. For variety, use a prerecorded Bible story and let the children pantomime the action and dialogue. Children like to make up their own songs, so let them write a song about the Bible story. Older children could make up modern parables to parallel those Jesus told.

## USING MUSIC

Music is a powerful medium of communication. It can entertain, arouse, calm, and control. It can be used as a means of instruction, worship, and expression. In teaching children, you can use music in several ways.

1. *Signal a change in activity.* Play a certain song on the piano or tape recorder in a preschool class to denote the end of playtime, the beginning of storytime, or the end of the class period.

2. *Create a special mood or atmosphere.* Use lively songs to welcome the students into the classroom. Use quieter music to prepare them for worship. Play different types of background music during prayer time or handwork activities.

3. *Spark discussion.* After listening to an excerpt of sacred or secular music, have the students discuss its meaning and effect. Help older children begin to understand the impact of secular music and to be discriminating in what they listen to.

4. *Develop personal musical talents.* Ask any students who are taking lessons to present special music for the class or

department. Also encourage the children to develop their song-writing abilities.

Keep the following principles in mind when planning to use music in your teaching:

1. *Strive for balance.* Choose songs of worship, testimony, and commitment. Include gospel songs and choruses, Scripture songs and hymns.

2. *Strive for variety.* Vary the tempo, rhythm, and style of music. Use a mix of familiar and new songs. Keep a record of the songs you sing and check to see that you are not overusing any.

3. *Strive for coordination.* Fit the songs to each other and to the theme of the session or service. Each song, like every other part of your lesson, should contribute to the accomplishment of your aims. Do not use music as a time filler.

4. *Strive for quality.* Ask yourself these questions about the music you use: Is the meaning of the words clear? Can the students understand the experiences expressed in the song? Is the song an accurate expression of God's Word? Does the music fit the words? Is the melody singable?

In selecting music for preschoolers, choose songs with no more than two to four lines. Repetitive songs work well with this age-group, particularly those that can be sung several ways by changing a few words. Choose songs with a simple melody line and keep the range from B to D. Instrumental accompaniment is not always necessary in singing with pre-schoolers. They enjoy playing rhythm band instruments as they sing, and they like to sing along with taped music.

Teach older children to appreciate all types of church music. Study the great hymns and their authors. Explain the doctrinal meaning of the songs they sing. Let the students write their own songs. Encourage them to dedicate their musical talents to the Lord. As previously suggested, have the students present special music, but first be sure they possess a certain degree of proficiency. Explain that God expects us to do our best when we sing or play for Him.

You may want to organize a children's choir to teach music-ministry fundamentals at an early age. Gospel Publishing House has a children's music section in their free catalog. Write to Gospel Publishing House, 1445 Boonville Avenue, Springfield, Missouri 65802–1894.

## USING PICTURES

Flat pictures serve many important purposes in teaching. They can be used to visualize a story or to clarify a verbal description. Pictures make things seem real. They are inexpensive and can be used in a variety of settings with no need for special equipment. On the other hand, pictures lack depth and motion and may be too small to use effectively with larger groups.

Two types of pictures may be used in Christian education, those prepared specifically for use in the church and those from other sources, such as magazines, calendars, newspapers, catalogs, postcards, advertisements, pamphlets, and take-home papers.

When selecting pictures ask yourself the following questions:

1. Will the picture contribute to the teaching-learning process?
2. Is the picture reliable? Does it tell the truth?
3. Is the picture interesting? Does it stimulate imagination and show action?
4. Does the picture have a clear-cut center of interest? Does it have good organization? Does it make effective use of color?
5. Is the picture suitable for my age-group? Is it related to my students' interests?

Pictures for younger children should portray objects and activities that are familiar to them. They should be simple and contain relatively little detail. The amount of detail may increase with the age of the children, with more complex pictures for older children, youth, and adults.

Properly mount and file pictures to enhance their usefulness. Make temporary mounts from colored construction paper, and more permanent mounts from poster board or cardboard. A background mount that picks up a dominant color in the picture will help lead the viewer's eye to the center of interest. Rubber cement is a good adhesive to use in mounting pictures because it can be removed without damaging either the picture or the mount. Spray a clear lacquer over the picture, or cover it with plastic wrap, to protect it from dirt and wear.

Begin with a simple picture-filing system. A large sturdy box will do for starters. As your collection grows, divide the pictures into categories, using cardboard dividers or file folders to separate them. Store smaller pictures in a standard filing cabinet or box. Store larger pictures vertically.

Use pictures as aids in telling Bible, missionary, or character stories, to review and introduce new ideas, to apply scriptural truth to life, and to teach memory verses or new songs. Include pictures in interest centers, on posters, and on bulletin boards.

## For Further Study

1. Why are children today under such intense pressure to grow up?
2. How can you more effectively train and equip parents to do a better job of raising their children?
3. Which of the five characteristics of children discussed in this chapter are exhibited most clearly in the children you teach?
4. What one thing can you do to improve your storytelling techniques?
5. How can you use music more effectively in your teaching?
6. What have you found to be a good source of pictures for teaching?

### NOTES

[1]George Barna, *The Frog in the Kettle* (Ventura, Calif.: Regal Books, 1990), 67,68.

[2]Martha Hamilton and Mitch Weiss, "A Teacher's Guide to Storytelling," *Instructor,* May/June 1991, 27–31.

# 9

# Providing Bible Teaching
# for Older Learners
# (Youth and Adult)

Today's youth live in a changing world, vastly different from the days when you were their age. Young people are staying home longer, living with their parents as they attend college or start a career. They are marrying at an older age (almost 3 years later than in the 1970s).

Puberty is occurring at a younger age, 2 to 5 years earlier than it did a century ago. And teens are becoming sexually active at an earlier age. In the general teen population, sexual intercourse is experienced for the first time around age 16.

This is also the most affluent generation of youth that has ever lived. According to George Barna, one-third of all teenagers who have reached driving age own a car. As a group, young people receive an annual income of $50 to $55 billion.[1]

Young people are greatly influenced by the media. By the time a teenager graduates from high school, he will have spent 10 years of 40-hour weeks watching television. During that time he will have seen 150,000 acts of violence, including 25,000 murders, and will have viewed 350,000 commercials. Music, movie, and television stars are the prime models for most children and youth.

## Understanding Today's Youth

Today's youth are much more pessimistic about life than previous generations were. For many young people, the future looks dismal. They have genuine concerns about getting a good job and establishing a career and have been told to lower their expectations. This pessimistic trend is seen in the dramatic rise in teen suicides (the second-highest cause of death among high school and college youth) and in the doom-and-gloom tone of much of today's popular music.

Today's youth are more conservative than their predecessors were and are more likely to follow their parents' faith and values. But the generation gap still exists, as young people struggle for independence from and acceptance by the adult world. Interpersonal relationships are important to teens. Young people are fiercely loyal to their peer groups, which greatly influence them. Teens live in a love-hate relationship with adults, skeptical of their authority, but still needing and wanting their direction.

## Reaching and Teaching Teens

So how do you minister to this generation of young people? How can you reach and teach them? Youths' greatest need is for in-depth Bible study and discipleship. Just reaching young people with the gospel is not enough; they need help getting grounded and established in their faith. Teens today need systematic Bible study. They need to know what they believe and why, and they must be encouraged to take their stand in a world that is rapidly moving in another direction.

Teens also need opportunities to experience what they believe. They need a hands-on faith that can be tried in the furnace of life. The church, in its ministry to youth, must provide significant opportunities for their involvement and service. If youth fail (and they will), the church must provide a safe place for them to return to and encourage them to talk about and learn from their experiences.

Teens need a significant relationship with an adult other than their parents. Studies have indicated that who these persons are is more important than how old they are. A survey of high school students revealed that teachers in their forties and fifties were the ones the students were most likely to seek for personal advice and counsel. As a teacher, you could provide such a ministry and make a crucial difference in your students' lives.

Another effective avenue of ministry to teens is providing training and help for the parents. Most young people still consider their parents the most influential people in their lives and respect and appreciate their advice and counsel. But parents need training to do a better job with their teens. The church's teaching ministries can help meet this need.

## Ministering to Today's Adults

The most significant phenomenon to occur this century in the adult world was the arrival of the baby boomers, the generation born between 1945 and 1964. They have effectively divided the rest of the adult world into two groups—the older adults who came before them, and the twenty-something generation.

Each of the three groups has unique needs. In fact, the age of adulthood, stretching from the post-high-school graduate to the octogenarian, encompasses more changes in every dimension of life than from birth through adolescence. Each adult age-group has specialized sets of developmental tasks to work through.

*Young adults* are engaged in selecting a mate, starting a family, parenting children, managing a home, choosing a life occupation, and developing friendships. *Middle adults* are trying to establish a standard of living, to help their teens move on toward adulthood, to learn how to relate to their changing spouse, to deal with their aging parents, and to prepare for their own retirement. *Older adults* are learning to adjust to physical changes, to retirement, to living on a reduced income, to changes in living arrangements, and to their spouse's and their own eventual death. Each of these life stages presents unique challenges and opportunities to minister to adults and make a difference in their lives.

### REACHING AND TEACHING ADULTS

Adults are experiencing a renewed interest in the church

and its teaching ministries. One reason is their concern for their families' spiritual training. They realize they need help with their marriages and help in parenting. Often they become burned out with worldly ways and desire someone to help them teach a different set of values to their children.

A fluctuating economy brings insecurity about the future. When hard times hit, people become frightened and look for something that offers hope and lasting value, so they turn to the church.

Adults still seek spiritual reality and believe strongly in the supernatural. What they need is a personal encounter with the Living God so they can experience His presence in their lives.

## WHAT THEY ARE LOOKING FOR

The adults returning to the church seek different ministries.

1. *Adults want practical teaching that will help them function in life.* They want their faith to work at home and on the job, not just at church. Therefore, they desire basic principles that they can apply to specific situations. Focus on practical life-related Bible studies and teach your students how to correctly interpret the Scriptures for themselves.

2. *Adults want things done well.* They want to be part of a group that meets their needs with quality ministries. Adults expect the church to function with the same efficiency they see elsewhere in society. Their parents' motto was, Do the best you can with what you have. But this generation's motto is, A job worth doing is worth doing right. Therefore, to reach and to hold adults, you must plan well, study well, and deliver well.

3. *Adults want to develop quality relationships.* They consider relationships to be the most important dimension of life. In fact, today's adults measure life itself in terms of how they get along with others. In some cases, they want relationships to be so perfect, that when they can't work one out, they quit and try again with someone else. Adults want to experience their faith in company with others. They want to love, laugh, cry, pray, care, and share together. Focus your teaching on

such primary relationships as husband-wife, child-parent, and boss-employee. Try to develop a greater transparency and vulnerability, so your students can see how you function in these areas and how you handle your successes and failures.

4. *Adults want to participate in learning and in leadership.* Elmer Towns says they are into learning rather than teaching.[2] Therefore, use dialogue methods such as buzz groups, panels, and symposiums. Adults also want to have a voice in goal-setting, problem-solving, and decision-making. One way to get their input is to conduct frequent class surveys and questionnaires.

5. *Adults want innovative, flexible programming.* Anything that sounds old or traditional tends to turn them off. The challenge to leadership is to continue devising new ideas, new courses, new classes. At times it may be better to offer two 6- or 7-week courses instead of one 13-week course. Concentrated weekend seminars are another possibility. Courses on audio or videotape would make it possible for adults to study at their convenience.

6. *Adults want to know about spiritual gifts.* They cannot be motivated by guilt or persuasion, but they are interested in learning how to minister in their area of spiritual giftedness. They want to know what the task involves and what they must do to accomplish it. The obvious response is to offer classes and short-term seminars on the subject of ministry gifts. Also, when approaching adults about serving in some capacity, be sure you have a current job description in hand. Your recruitment appeal should focus on personal fulfillment, not on duty or obligation.

## More Methods for Youth and Adults

USING DISCUSSION

Discussion methods are some of the most effective ways to teach youth and adults. People like to talk, and this approach encourages them to do so productively. But occasionally you will hear a teacher ask, "How can I get my students to respond in class? I ask them questions and they just sit there."

If that happens to you, the first thing to do is to try to discover why your students will not talk. For some people, it may simply be a matter of conditioning. For years they were told to sit still and be quiet. Now, after a long time of adjusting to that, they are thoroughly conditioned to avoid participation.

For other students, the problem may be that their past participation was not always a positive experience. Maybe one or two students dominated the discussion, or sharp disagreements arose. At other times, the discussion may have reached no definite conclusions, and the students felt it was a frustrating waste of time. Perhaps they did venture an answer one time, but felt embarrassed because it was not the answer the teacher wanted. Now they remember the trite and often wrong cliche, "Better to remain silent and be thought a fool than to speak out and remove all doubt."

Sometimes discussion methods do not work well because the environment is not conducive. For example, many adult classes meet in the sanctuary. The arrangement of pews does not lend itself to interaction, and the room may be too big to hear others clearly.

With an understanding of the problems, let's look at some solutions.

1. Assure your students that you sincerely want their participation. This may take some time, but eventually your attitude and actions will convince them. Express your appreciation for all comments offered, especially those from someone who may not speak up very often.

2. When you do get a wrong response, try to use what is right about it and call on others for further information. Or simply say, "Well, that's something I've never thought of before. Does anyone else have a comment?" Sometimes it helps to take the blame for a poorly worded question. That way you don't make the student feel bad for giving an incorrect answer.

3. When you ask a question, wait several seconds before call-

ing on someone. If no answer is forthcoming, rephrase the question or answer it yourself. Remember, a thoughtful question calls for a thoughtful answer, so give the students time to think. Do not fear silence; it may be some of the most productive time in your classroom.

4. Take time beforehand to write discussion questions. Do not depend on the inspiration of the moment. Do not make the questions too simple, or you risk insulting the students' intelligence. Likewise, overly complex questions will not elicit a response. It is usually best to center the discussion on problems or issues your students can identify with and become personally involved in.

5. Plan a good introduction to the discussion. You may want to use an open-ended story, a case study, a current event, a roleplay, or an agree-disagree exercise.

6. As a teacher, it is your job to control the discussion. That means you are not obligated to provide a platform for an opinionated student. For the good of the class, you must control such students with all necessary restraint. Occasionally it may be necessary to remind them not to monopolize the discussion. At times it may be best to call on a specific individual or to simply say, "Let's hear from someone who hasn't said anything yet."

7. Choose your discussion methods carefully. If the students are reluctant to speak up, select several to serve on a panel. Provide them with a list of questions to review beforehand. If you have a large class, you may occasionally want to divide it into buzz groups of six to eight students. If your class meets in an auditorium, divide the students into dyads (pairs) for 2- to 3-minute discussions. Use the circle response or brainstorming technique when trying to garner a large number of responses. An agree-disagree exercise is a good way to introduce a topic and generate a lively discussion.

USING PROJECTS AND ASSIGNMENTS

Projects and assignments are effective ways to teach youth

and adults because they involve the students in direct learning activities and provide an outlet for expression and service. They also help develop leadership skills, promote cooperation and fellowship among the students, and make learning fun, interesting, and more lasting.

Findley Edge divides projects and assignments into four basic categories based on their learning objectives.[3]

1. *Information projects* lead the students to master certain information. Examples include researching historical backgrounds, surveying theological positions, presenting a book report, compiling a list of Bible verses on a particular topic, writing answers to a list of study questions, and compiling a scrapbook of notes taken during the quarter.

2. *Attitude projects* help the students to develop or to deepen certain attitudes. Examples include visiting a hospital or jail; touring a slum area; surveying the opinions of people in the class, the church, the school, or the workplace; and compiling a list of personal responses to an assigned Bible passage.

3. *Habit projects* help the students to develop or to change certain habits. Examples include initiating a campaign for class members to sit near the front of the sanctuary or to be more reverent in church, beginning a program of regular Bible reading, conducting a personal evaluation of an area of spiritual weakness, and making a list of prayer needs to remember during the coming week.

4. *Service projects* lead the students to render service to others, thereby giving expression to the Christian life. Examples include making gifts for shut-ins and missionaries, sponsoring a letter-writing campaign, carrying out a work project for the elderly, making improvements in and around the church, conducting services at a jail or rest home, and sponsoring a fund-raising project.

Numerous writing projects can be used with youth and adults.

1. *Sentence completion*—Give the students several state-

ments to complete, such as, "In class today I learned that . . . . This means I need to . . . . In the coming week I will . . . ."

2. *Personal evaluation*—Give the students a list of questions or statements to respond to. Some questions or statements may be answered on a continuum scale whereby the students indicate the degree of compliance or need. An example would be, "I read my Bible (5) every day, (4) usually every day, (3) frequently, (2) occasionally, (1) hardly ever."

3. *Art project*—Ask the students to make bumper stickers or campaign lapel pins, to draw a cartoon strip or graph, or to make a graffiti poster or time line.

4. *Log or diary*—Have the students compile either a personal diary or a diary that a Bible character, such as Daniel or Peter, might have written.

5. *Newspaper story*—Have the students write a news account or an ad as it might have appeared in a local news publication during Bible times.

6. *Paraphrase*—Ask the students to write a personal paraphrase of a brief Bible passage, putting its meaning in their own words.

7. *Letter*—Ask the students to write letters to themselves stating a spiritual goal they would like to achieve. Have them seal the letters, address the envelopes to themselves, and give them to you. Mail the letters during the week or at the end of the quarter.

8. *Sensory response*—Have the students read a Bible story and write down a color, smell, touch, taste, and sound the incident brings to mind. Ask each student to explain the reason for his selections.

9. *Acrostic*—Ask the students to develop an acrostic listing words or phrases beginning with each letter of a key word, such as *thanksgiving* or *liberty*.

USING CHARTS AND GRAPHS

Charts and graphs are useful teaching tools for youth and adults. They visually represent numerical and statistical data, revealing important trends and variations from the norm. There are several different types of graphs: line graphs drawn on a grid, bar graphs presenting comparisons and changes, and pie graphs showing the relationship of the parts to the whole. Use graphs to report on attendance, to compare income with expenses, to project church growth, etc.

A chart is a graphic display of words, numbers, or pictures. It can be as simple as a list of the books of the Bible, or as complex as a comparison of the reigns of the Old Testament kings with the ministry of the prophets. Charts are helpful in summarizing information, clarifying relationships, and portraying an idea visually.

There are many different kinds of charts. An *outline chart* organizes content into main points and subpoints and is very useful in teaching. An *organizational chart* shows functional relationships. It gives a good overall picture of a program or organization. *Diagrams* are also a type of chart. They are condensed drawings representing such items as an area, an outline, and key features. A *time line chart* shows a sequence of events and the relationship of the events to each other. It is a way of visualizing a specific time span.

Charts can be used in a number of ways to teach youth and adults. For example, use a chart to outline a book of the Bible, to list the main points of a Bible study, or to diagram a Scripture passage. Use a flip chart to tell a Bible story or to illustrate the sequence of end-time events. Use a grid chart to explain the threefold work of Christ as prophet, priest, and king.

## For Further Study

1. How do today's youth differ from preceding generations?
2. How can you give your young people more opportunities to put their faith into practice?
3. What impact has the baby boom generation had on our world? on our church? Has it been positive or negative?
4. What changes should the church make to minister more effectively to adults?

5. What discussion methods work best with your group?
6. What writing projects have you tried with your group?
7. Why are graphs and charts effective tools for teaching youth and adults?

## NOTES

[1]George Barna, *The Frog in the Kettle* (Ventura, Calif.: Regal Books, 1990), 70.

[2]Elmer Towns, *How To Reach the Baby Boomer* (Lynchburg, Va.: Church Growth Institute, 1990), 40.

[3]Findley B. Edge, *Helping the Teacher* (Nashville, Tenn.: Broadman Press, 1959), 128,129.

# 10

## The Priorities of Bible Teaching

It is possible for you to know all about the techniques of effective Bible teaching and to still miss the priorities on which it is based: keeping the Bible the centerpiece of your ministry, and constantly striving to bring your students into a personal relationship with Jesus Christ as their Savior and Lord. These priorities make a difference for all eternity.

### Keeping the Focus on the Bible

How much class time did your students spend last week in actual Bible study? Much of what happens in the classroom does not involve the use of the Bible. For the Bible to be truly your teaching textbook, you must make greater use of it in the classroom.

Effective use of the Bible begins with your example. Your students should see you and other staff members bringing Bibles to class and to church. Occasionally share with your students how you read the Bible devotionally and in preparation for your teaching assignments. Also show proper respect for the Bible, handling it reverently and turning the pages carefully. Do not pile books and other papers on top of the Bible. Through your example, even young children who are still unable to read will learn proper respect for the Word. Another way to teach respect for God's Word is to prominently display a large Bible in your classroom or department area.

The classroom is also a good place to teach the importance of daily personal devotions. Promote a Bible-reading program to encourage Bible reading outside the class. Make assignments for the coming week and keep a record of the students' Bible reading on a chart in your classroom. Memory work can also be a part of the program. Give appropriate recognition and awards to the students who complete the program.

The Bible will become more meaningful as your students understand its history, organization, and structure. Explain how we got our Bibles. Help younger students learn the books of the Bible and the major divisions in the Old and New Testaments. Help older students to understand how the different parts of the Bible relate to one another. For example, knowing how the Old Testament prophets fit into the history of Israel and Judah would be helpful. The Epistles could be studied in relationship to the churches or the individuals to whom they were addressed.

Older children, youth, and adults need to learn such Bible-study basics as the deductive and inductive approaches. The deductive method begins with an idea or doctrine, then goes to the Bible for support. The inductive approach begins with a Bible passage before formulating any conclusions. Other Bible-study methods the students should learn are the topical, biographical, historical, and grammatical methods. After studying these methods under your guidance and encouragement, your students can then use them at home.

Your students should also learn how to use margin cross-references, how to find Bible locations on a map, and how to use a concordance, a Bible dictionary (for looking up unfamiliar words or ideas), and a Bible handbook (for learning background information on different Bible books).

Perhaps the most common method of using the Bible in the classroom is reading the text for the day's lesson. To prevent this from becoming a perfunctory practice, try varying your approach.

1. Have the students read in unison.
2. Have a student read the entire passage.
3. Have a responsive reading.

4. Have two or more students read the dialogue, with a narrator filling in the details.

5. Set up a choral reading, assigning group and solo parts.

6. Have the students read the same verses from different versions or paraphrases.

7. Play the assigned passage on a cassette tape.

## TEN WAYS TO INCLUDE THE BIBLE IN YOUR TEACHING

1. *Setting Bible verses to music*—The Bible becomes more interesting and is more easily remembered when portions are put to music and songs are based on biblical settings and events. Use Bible songs to introduce the lesson, to learn the memory verse, or to conclude the lesson. Let the students make up their own melodies for selected verses. Use records or cassette tapes of Scripture songs and choruses.

2. *Using quizzes*—Use written and oral quizzes to review the Bible content of previous lessons, to generate class participation, and to motivate lesson study. Let the students make up their own questions to ask one another. Introduce them to the Junior and Teen Bible Quiz programs, and sponsor competitions.

3. *Playing Bible games*—Games are a fun way to help your students become familiar with Bible facts, people, places, and events. Make up your own simple games, such as "Who Am I?" or "Who Said It?" or adapt games such as Bible baseball, sword drills, crossword puzzles, or charades. Many TV game shows can be adapted as Bible-learning activities. And Bible versions of many popular games, such as Bible Trivia and Bible Pictionary, are also available.

4. *Marking Bible passages*—The Bible will become more meaningful to your students if they mark significant passages. Encourage them to underscore verses with a pen or pencil or to shade them lightly with a pencil, highlighting pen, or colored pencils. Different colors can serve as codes for specific topics: red for salvation, blue for heaven, green for healing, etc. Mark

memory verses for younger children so they can find them during the week.

5. *Making chain references*—Help older students to select several topics, such as salvation, the Holy Spirit, or faith, and to develop a chain reference for those topics in their Bibles. A chain reference is made by writing the second reference next to the first verse, the third reference next to the second verse, etc. Such a system is perfect to use in witnessing when explaining the plan of salvation. Provide study resources, such as a concordance or chain-reference Bible.

6. *Memorizing Scripture passages*—With young children, use short, simple verses or verse portions. Be sure to explain any words the children may not understand. Take time to review the verses your students have previously learned. Younger elementary children can learn one new verse a week, while older elementary children can undertake a more extensive memory program. Encourage them to learn longer portions, such as the Lord's Prayer, the Beatitudes, and Psalm 23. Encourage youth and adults to continue memorizing the Scriptures. To facilitate study, provide them with pocket-sized cards to write Bible verses on.

7. *Paraphrasing Scripture passages*—Have older students write a passage in their own words. This technique helps the students to think through the meaning of the passage and gets them actively involved in the lesson.

8. *Hand-copying Scripture passages*—Set a goal for your class or department to copy a certain Bible portion. Encourage individual students to sign up for part of the assigned portion. Provide paper and pencils or let each student choose his own type and size of paper. You may want to present the completed portion to the pastor in a church service.

9. *Making Bible tapes*—Choose a Bible book or passage and have each student sign up to read part of it into a tape recorder. Older children or youth classes may want to try making a dramatized Bible tape complete with narrator, speaking parts, and sound effects.

10. *Having group studies*—This technique works well with

older children, youth, and adults. Divide the class into groups of four to six students. Explain the background of the Bible passage and supply each group with several leading questions, such as, To whom was the passage written? Why? When? What conditions of that time parallel today's? How can we carry out the passage's teaching? Allow 5 to 10 minutes, then ask each group to give a report. This method helps the students learn good principles of Bible study that they can use in their personal study.

## Keeping the Focus on Evangelism

A survey of 300 churches in 12 states revealed a disconcerting fact: over one-half of the teachers surveyed had not led one soul to Christ in the past year. Evangelism in the classroom was simply not happening.

### PROBLEMS AND PRINCIPLES

Most Christian educators would agree the classroom is an ideal setting for leading people to Christ, but it does present problems that can hinder the work of evangelism. For example, your students may demonstrate a wide range of spiritual understanding and needs. Some students may know the Bible well, while others lack understanding of even the simplest biblical teachings.

Some students may respond to every invitation, feeling they need to get saved again every time they do something wrong. Children may respond to an invitation simply to please their leader, because they are tired of sitting, or because others are responding. On the other hand, youth and adults may not respond because others are not responding. Children may fail to understand some of the symbolic or abstract terms you use to explain the salvation experience. They can easily become overstimulated and respond out of extreme fear of punishment.

The following principles can help you to overcome these problems:

1. *Keep it simple.* Avoid abstract and symbolic terms that may not be understood. Keep the message as literal as possible.

2. *Ask questions to find out why your students have responded to the invitation.* Try to determine their understanding of the salvation experience. Explain the difference between being saved and asking forgiveness for doing something wrong. Stress that salvation is based on what the Bible says, not on feelings.

3. *Stress the love of God.* When inviting your students to accept Christ, avoid an overly emotional appeal, especially when working with children. They need to know God loves them and wants them to become part of His family.

4. *Deal with your students individually.* In the classroom setting, mass evangelism is not as effective as the individual approach. Talk personally with each student to determine his needs and his understanding of salvation.

5. *Require action that is contrary to nature.* Instead of asking those who want to receive Christ to come forward, ask them to remain seated and dismiss the rest of the group. The students will be less likely to respond to Christ simply because of peer pressure.

PRESENTING THE GOSPEL TO YOUNG CHILDREN

Ministry to the cradle-roll child, of course, focuses on evangelizing the parents. Take this opportunity to make them aware of how important they are to their child's spiritual development. Conversions can occur in the preschool years, but they are the exception, not the rule. Therefore, lay a foundation on which future experiences can be built. Help preschoolers to understand that God loves them, that Jesus is God's Son, that He came to be their friend and helper, and that Jesus is sad when they do wrong. Be alert to and deal individually with the inquisitive child who shows interest in knowing more about receiving Christ.

## PRESENTING THE GOSPEL TO ELEMENTARY CHILDREN

Many early elementary children will be able to understand the gospel and respond to it, but some may still not be ready. By the time the children reach the older elementary years, every child should be ready for a conversion experience. In fact, this period is often called the golden age of child evangelism.

The following chart explains how to approach early and older elementary children:

| EARLY ELEMENTARY (ages 6 to 8) | OLDER ELEMENTARY (ages 9 to 11) |
|---|---|
| Stress the love of God | Stress God's justice and fairness |
| Talk about becoming a member of God's family | Talk about making decisions for life and eternity |
| Use simple, literal language | Use more abstractions and symbolisms |
| Use a single story or illustration | Use illustrations that stress action and adventure |

## THE AGE OF ACCOUNTABILITY

Several factors determine when a child becomes accountable before God for his salvation.

1. *Home background*—A child from a Christian home will understand spiritual things more quickly than a child from an unchurched family. He will also have more opportunities to respond to Christ.

2. *Mental maturity*—Although salvation is not a matter of intellect alone, some basic facts do need to be understood. A child who is mentally advanced will grasp these concepts sooner and will realize his need of salvation at an earlier age.

3. *Spiritual sensitivity*—Some children are more spiritually sensitive than others, perhaps due to one of the other two fac-

tors. Such a child will respond more readily than someone who is not as sensitive.

### PRESENTING THE GOSPEL TO YOUTH

Youth is a time of questioning and decision. Teens are concerned about their identity, acceptance, and response to peer pressure versus adult pressure. Many are aware there is more to life than just accumulating things or gaining popularity. Young people are looking for direction and will respond to loving, understanding leadership. Your approach should be to recognize them as people of decision and to help them find their identity as loved and accepted people.

Young people are sometimes embarrassed to show emotion or to be singled out and put on the spot. Therefore, a personal approach is often more effective than a group appeal. Do not try to force young people into a salvation experience. Instead, ask the Lord to help you develop a sensitivity to the Holy Spirit and trust Him to do His work His way.

### PRESENTING THE GOSPEL TO ADULTS

Adults are the leaders of the home, of business, and of the community. When we win adults, we often win entire families. Adults both inside and outside the church are searching for reality. They are concerned about goals, relationships, family needs, and the future. However, some barriers to accepting salvation are ingrained habits and life-styles, a hardening of the heart, a failure to attend church, a limited spiritual understanding, and an unwillingness to change.

Adults are more likely to respond to someone who has gained their trust, someone whom they consider a friend. Help them to understand that accepting Christ will improve their relationships, especially with their families. Let them know both the benefits of salvation and the cost of following Christ. Do not try to threaten or pressure adults to make a decision; coercion is not necessary. When the Holy Spirit has done the work, the decision will be sound and lasting.

Your approach to adults and to youth should be made on a threefold basis:
1. *Intellect*—Recognition of sin and acceptance of salvation by faith
2. *Emotions*—Sorrow for sin and love and trust in God
3. *Will*—Renunciation of sin and a determination to follow Christ

## PRINCIPLES FOR COUNSELING AND FOLLOW-UP

When a student approaches you about becoming a Christian or responds to an invitation in class or church, follow these principles.

1. *Establish rapport.* Call the student by his first name. Smile and look pleased about his response.

2. *Ask several questions to determine the student's understanding of the plan of salvation.* Find out why he responded to the invitation or appeal. Ask him if he knows what it means to receive Christ as his Savior.

3. *Use a few Bible verses to point out the way of salvation.* If you are speaking to a child, use only one or two verses, such as John 3:16, 1 John 1:9, or Revelation 3:20.

4. *Encourage the student to pray a simple prayer of repentance, asking Christ to come into his life.* You may have to suggest several things he should say, but try to avoid the repeat-after-me prayer. Help the student to understand that prayer is simply talking to God and requires no previous experience.

5. *After the student has prayed, ask several questions to determine the impact and reality of his experience.* Review the plan of salvation if you are not sure that he understands. Help him to base his faith on what the Bible says, not on his feelings. Pray for the student, thanking God for saving him. In this way you begin affirming his experience.

6. *Record the date of the student's conversion.* If he has a Bible, have him write the date on the flyleaf. That will help underscore the significance of his life-changing experience.

7. *As you leave the classroom or altar area, look for someone the student can share his experience with.* It should be someone who will rejoice with him, such as another teacher or the pastor. This will be the student's first opportunity to give witness to his faith in Christ.

8. *Give the student brief instructions on the need for prayer, Bible reading, daily cleansing, and witnessing.* Mark several verses in his Bible for him, including the ones you shared with him. Suggest he begin his Bible reading with the Book of Mark.

9. *Help the student to understand that conversion is the beginning of a life of service to Christ.* If he attends your class, give him a special task to do.

10. *If the student is a child, talk to his family as soon as possible about the decision he has made.* Be alert to opportunities to lead any unsaved family members to Christ. Provide the student with copies of any follow-up or study materials your church may have available.

## For Further Study

1. By your example, what important lessons can you teach your students about respecting the Bible?
2. How can you train your students in the use of Bible-study helps?
3. How can you motivate your students to memorize more Scripture passages?
4. What problems do you sometimes encounter in trying to lead your students to accept Christ as their Savior?
5. At what age do you think children become personally accountable before God for their salvation?
6. Why is it important that you reach adults with the gospel?

# Bibliography

Allen, R. R., S. Anderson, and others *Speech in American Society.* Columbus, Ohio: Charles E. Merrill Publishing Co., 1968.

Barna, George. *The Frog in the Kettle.* Ventura, Calif.: Regal Books, 1990.

Bell, A. Donald. *How To Get Along With People in the Church.* Grand Rapids, Mich.: Zondervan Publishing House, 1960.

Brendel, Doug, and others. *Way To Grow.* Springfield, Mo.: National Sunday School Department, Assemblies of God, 1981.

Byrne, Herbert W. *Christian Education for the Local Church.* Grand Rapids, Mich.: Zondervan Publishing House, 1963.

Collins, Gary. *How To Be a People Helper.* Santa Ana, Calif.: Vision House, 1976.

Davis, Billie. *Teaching To Meet Crisis Needs.* Springfield, Mo.: Gospel Publishing House, 1984.

Edge, Findley B. *Helping the Teacher.* Nashville, Tenn.: Broadman Press, 1959.

_____. *Teaching for Results.* Nashville, Tenn.: Broadman Press, 1956.

"Editorial Perspective," *Ministries Today* 8, (November/December 1990).

Ezell, Mancil. *Making Nonprojected Visuals and Displays.* Nashville, Tenn.: Broadman Press, 1975.

Hamilton, Martha, and Mitch Weiss. "A Teacher's Guide to Story-telling," *Instructor* (May/June 1991).

Hendrix, Olan. *Management for the Christian Worker.* Santa Barbara, Calif.: Quill Publications, 1976.

Rexroat, Stephen. *The Sunday School Spirit.* Springfield, Mo.: Gospel Publishing House, 1979.

Richards, Lawrence O. *Creative Bible Teaching.* Chicago, Ill.: Moody Press, 1970.

————. *You, the Teacher.* Chicago, Ill.: Moody Press, 1972.

Towns, Elmer. *How To Reach the Baby Boomer.* Lynchberg, Va.: Church Growth Institute, 1990.

Waitley, Denis. *10 Seeds of Greatness.* Old Tappan, N.J.: Fleming H. Revell Company, 1983.

Wilhoit, Jim, and Leland Ryken. *Effective Bible Teaching.* Grand Rapids, Mich.: Baker Book House, 1988.

Wright, H. Norman. *So You're Getting Married.* Ventura, Calif.: Regal Books, 1985.